DOUBLE YOUR MONEY IN ANTIQUES IN 60 DAYS

Books by George Grotz:

FROM GUNK TO GLOW

THE FURNITURE DOCTOR

THE NEW ANTIQUES

ANTIQUES YOU CAN DECORATE WITH

INSTANT FURNITURE REFINISHING

STAINING AND REFINISHING UNFINISHED FURNITURE AND OTHER NAKED WOODS

DECORATING FURNITURE WITH A LITTLE CLASS

THE ANTIQUE RESTORER'S HANDBOOK

THE CURRENT ANTIQUE FURNITURE STYLE & PRICE GUIDE

THE FUN OF REFINISHING FURNITURE

GROTZ'S 2ND ANTIQUE FURNITURE STYLE & PRICE GUIDE

GROTZ'S DECORATIVE COLLECTIBLES PRICE GUIDE

Double Your Money in Antiques in 60 Days

And Other Secrets of the Antiques Business

by
GEORGE GROTZ
author of *The Furniture Doctor*

DOUBLEDAY & COMPANY, INC.
Garden City, New York
1986

Library of Congress Cataloging-in-Publication Data

Grotz, George.
Double your money in antiques in 60 days.

Bibliography: p. 171.
1. Antiques as an investment. I. Title.
NK1125.G764 1986 332.63 85-10280
ISBN 0-385-19515-X

PRINTED IN THE UNITED STATES OF AMERICA

CONTENTS

PART II

The 45 Fastest-selling Antiques that You Can Buy and Sell for a Quick Profit

PART III

24 Things Not to Buy

APPENDIX

PREFACE: THE DUMB AND THE RICH

Or, how to double your money in antiques every sixty days as a full-time dealer or just having fun on weekends

Do you really want to get rich in antiques? Or at least make some real money for a change? Well, then just listen to me because in the last thirty years I've seen it all in the Wonderful World of Antiques. And one of the things that I have seen is that the vast majority of antique dealers are just plain dumb. And on the lower end of the scale some are even stupid. While at the top you have the few smart ones who make lots of money.

So over my years in this business—getting rich writing, because I am not one of the vast majority of dumb writers—I have been observing this phenomenon and figuring out what makes the difference between these three kinds of antique dealers. The stupid, who *lose* money. The vast majority of the dumb ones, who just make a few dollars once in a while. And the few rich ones, who know the secrets of how to double their money every sixty days. (Specifically, we're talking about doubling about $10,000 every sixty days, and that's a yearly income of $60,000, which is rich enough for me. And we are talking about country-living dealers without any big-city shops. In fact, often with no shop at all—just a big station wagon and a small storage barn.)

How do they do it? By not being dumb, but smart. And the difference is that the dumb dealer is a romantic, and the smart dealer is a realist.

The romantic dealers think that antiques are swell. Interesting reminders of our cultural past. Quaint. Artistic. Sophisticated. Worth cataloging and knowing about in infinite detail. And worst of all, that everything that is antique is worth the time it takes to buy and sell it. Wow! Has the dumb romantic dealer got a wrong number.

The romantic dealer thinks that if he doubles his investment on interesting little objects in the $2–$5–$10–$15–$20 class he is making money. And he isn't. All he is doing is providing an interesting browsing experience for people who don't have much else to do.

The romantic dealer buys wicker chaise lounges painted white ("Everybody loves them these days"). When he could fit four much sought-after ladies' desks in the same space and double six to eight times as much money. He's a loser—and he doesn't even know it. Or why.

But never again need you be a loser, Dear Reader, once you have learned all the secrets of the realistic dealers that are crammed into the following pages of this book.

Like what to buy. And where to buy. And when to sell. And where to sell. And all these secrets can be

SMART PEOPLE

VARIOUS KINDS OF DUMB PEOPLE

PROPORTION OF SMART PEOPLE IN THE GENERAL POPULATION

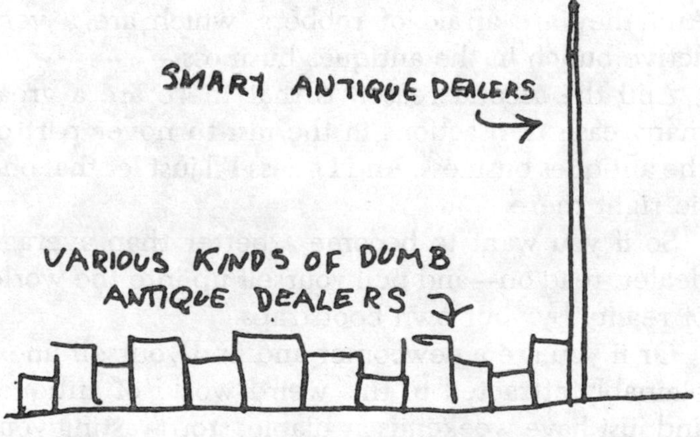

PROPORTION OF SMART PEOPLE AMONG ANTIQUE DEALERS

used by people who just want to have fun doubling their money on weekends going to auctions and flea markets, as well as people who want to run a full-time business with a big station wagon and a little storage barn.

And all this is real. Real and true. Because everything I write about, I have seen happen. And it is happening right now, and I can take you to the places where it is going on and show it to you.

Then why have I concealed the identities of these successful/realistic people who know how to make a lot of money in antiques? For two very good reasons. The first is that these people want no publicity at all except in the trade press—and not much there—because their homes usually contain a fortune in the "good stuff" that they have skimmed off the surface of the things that have passed through their hands. And they are afraid of robbers, which are a very active bunch in the antiques business.

And the second reason is that there are a great many cash transactions in the fast-turnover part of the antiques business. And I guess I'll just let that one lie right there.

So if you want to become a better than average dealer, read on—and pull yourself up into the world of reality by your own bootstraps.

Or if you are a newcomer and find yourself unexplainably attracted to this weird world of antiques and just have weekends available, stop wasting your time playing tennis and jogging and all those dumb things. First, read this true book about reality. And then get out in the Wonderful World of Antiques and double your money every sixty days. The way smart people do.

In the first section of this book, I'm going to let you in on some of the truths and secrets I've learned over the years. Good stuff on just what it takes to be a winner. Then after I tell you "how," I'm going to reveal to you "with what." This is the real lowdown on the hottest items to buy and, equally as important, a no-no list of what not to touch.

Part I

HOW THE ANTIQUES BUSINESS WORKS

My Wife and the Harvard School of Business Administration

Or, why people who don't pay attention end up being poor all their lives

My wife doesn't like the title of this book. She says that nobody will believe me when I say that you can sell an antique for twice what you paid for it in only sixty days.

But that's not what I said!!!!!!

That would just be a lucky break, meaning you'd have to be lucky to buy way below market value or sell way above market value, as at some turkey-shoot —which is what they call those summer auctions up in New England where they get all those rich city lawyers and doctors who come up on weekends to visit their rich city kids at camp.

What I am talking about is fast turnover of invested capital. And in this case we are talking about turning that capital over every two weeks, or four times in sixty days. Which means you need only make a 25 percent profit each time to have doubled your original investment in eight weeks or sixty days. And that is why we only buy the fastest-moving object that we can be sure of reselling in two weeks. Got it? Or do I have to send you to the Harvard School of Business Administration, too!

But, you say, I can't sell an antique in two weeks. And I say, the hell you can't! You could do it in four days if you moved fast enough back and forth between flea markets and antique dealers and got a little lucky about finding fast sellers, which you often can find even in one antique shop, and which you then dump off in the next—even if only at a 10 percent profit.

Which brings up the point. What we are talking about is an average profit of 25 percent. If you make a mistake, and two dealers turn your object down at your 25 percent markup, don't hold out. Just see if you can unload it for what you paid for it right away. Money tied up in a nonseller will never make you any profit. You should even lose money on it if you have to in order to get your money into something else. And fast for that, too. And mark it up to experience—you just found out about something you should never buy again. Turn over. Turnover. That's the whole secret. And to tell you the truth, if I weren't afraid of my little old wife, I would have called this book *Double Your Money in 30 Days in Antiques.* It is really so easy once you get rid of that shopkeeper syndrome that dominates all those losers out there with their dingy little antique shops full of unsalable historic relics that they have been moving around from table to shelf for years while the money invested in their stock would be making them more in a savings bank account. If they have saving banks anymore.

But getting back to the percentages of profit. There is another aspect of this turnover trading that I guess I am going to have to cover even though it should be obvious even to those of you with the meanest intelligence. And this is, that you have to make a percentage on a significant amount of investment to get any significant return in relationship to the time you have spent in this given activity.

LADIES' WALL DESK
OPEN

LADIES' WALL DESK
CLOSED

In somewhat plainer English, this means that you can't mess around with little $2 and $3 objects even if you are sure you can triple your money in them, because for the time it takes you, all you are making is peanuts. Nor can you afford to waste any time with $5 and $10 objects. Now where exactly the worth-your-time price range begins is hard to say, but I can tell you this: the most successful operators prefer to deal in small pieces of antique furniture if it is available—anything that will fit in a station wagon. So here you are talking about, say, one of those thin oak wall desks with some applied carving on the front and a little bevel-edged curvy mirror on the top. Well, the fair price range would be for you to pay $150 for it, for a dealer you know who wants them to pay you $200 for it and for the dealer to sell it at $250 to $275 to his customer. And for all of these sales to take place in a week because dealers have ladies waiting for them to have such a desk, ladies' desks being one of the fastest movers in antiques.

Well, in this case—and it is a quite ordinary one—you have already made 33 percent on your money in a few days. The idea is to multiply this operation as many times as you can in sixty, and if you haven't doubled your money by then, you just haven't been trying. And you are not doubling nickels and dimes.

In fact, the higher the price range, the better. And when you get up to buying desks for $600 and selling them quickly for only $750, you are in the class of the kind of dealers who after five years experience in the business are making $40,000 and up.

And don't tell me that you're not a natural salesman, because the operation we are talking about here isn't selling. It is *supplying*—the needs of dealers who are waiting for you to come or even telephone them that you have something for them. This isn't "selling." It's filling a need.

Of course, I have kept this whole discussion in terms of buying from a flea market and selling to a dealer with whom you have made previous contact, so that you know what he is looking for and *needs*. Naturally, there are other ways to operate. Such as buying from the wholesalers, at auctions and contents of houses from banks to name a few. I'll go into these operations in other chapters, but for now I only want you to understand the basic economics of the profit margin involved in the fast turnover of capital.

Learn what's in demand, preferably easily portable items, in price ranges where a reasonable profit of 25 to 30 percent on a quick turnover is worthwhile. I don't think my wife gets it yet, but that's my problem and not yours. Maybe she could go up to Boston this winter and take a couple of courses at the Harvard Business School.

Where the Antiques Come From

The source areas for $20 billion worth of "virgin" American antiques just waiting for you

Every once in a while I run into some know-it-all twit who tells me, "You can't find any good antiques any more." Baloney. There are literally millions of old homes out there that still contain the stuff they were originally furnished with over a hundred to two hundred years ago. And if there are only two million, with *only* $10,000 worth of stuff in them, that's $20 billion worth waiting to drop into your hands like a ripe peach.

Where, you say? Well, I'll tell you exactly where:

In the western half of New York State.

In northeastern New York State, north of Albany. (Can you think of the name of a single city or town in either of those two vast areas that industrial development has passed by? And they are packed with old farmhouses!)

And it is the same lonely, desolate way in western Pennsylvania, western Virginia and southern Ohio.

Also across the northern halves of Vermont, New

Hampshire and Maine—in fact, almost any part of Maine more than five miles inland from the coast.

And even in the areas of eastern Connecticut, Rhode Island and southeastern Massachusetts.

But how do you get them, you say? One answer, as morbid as it may seem, is that you wait for the old folks in those houses to die. At which point, estates must be settled and the contents of those houses are auctioned off the following summer (and some in the spring and fall) so that the grandchildren who have moved to the city can split the loot.

And, of course, you find out about these auctions in the trade press of the antiques business, which is fully discussed in another chapter.

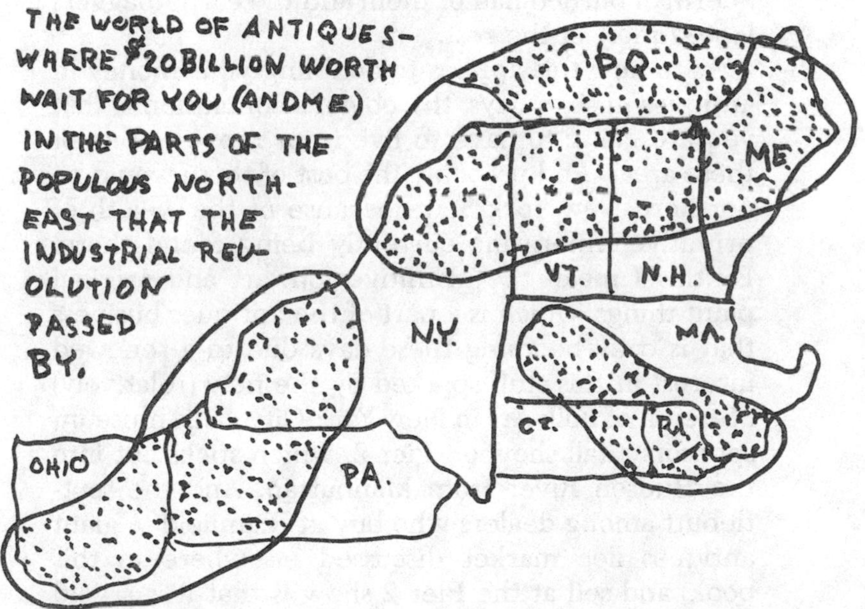

To make all this "perfectly clear," as our former President with the moral vacuum used to say, I have drawn a map, which I must say surprises me—in that there is so much of this territory. But on the other hand, consider how much of the United States I have left off the map. But that is because when you stop to think about it, the rest of the United States is all new and doesn't have any antiques because nobody was there to have anything to get old and become an antique.

Except the South, you say. But the trouble with the South is that, being mostly rural, there was hardly anybody there, with the exception of Virginia. And in Georgia the only objects of value were in the widely scattered plantation mansions and General Sherman burned half of them and the carpetbaggers looted most of the rest.

As to how this applies to doubling your money in antiques in sixty days, the obvious conclusion is that you are going to have to live in or move to one of these areas. And probably the best of them would be northern New York State because of the wealth of primitive Americana currently being found there. By this I mean the primitive folk art and original paint things, which is a part of the antiques business that is truly booming these days due to a renewed interest in this stuff sparked by the new (relatively) Museum of Folk Art in New York City. This museum sponsors a fall show on Pier 2, which sticks out into the Hudson River from Manhattan. And the scuttlebutt among dealers who buy at Brimfield (a giant antiques flea market discussed elsewhere in this book) and sell at the Pier 2 show is that it is a gold mine. According to one dealer, "Those New Yorkers rush into the show with fistfuls of hundred dollar bills, and they will buy *anything*—faster than you can raise the prices on your junk." And another dealer chimes in (this was at the little town coffee shop in Brimfield, Mass.), "You mean anything with old paint on it." And another voice says, "You mean if it's got blue paint on it, that dusty powder blue, it drives them out of their minds! [Pause.] Anybody want to buy a quart of it? I mixed up too much of it last week."

Oh, some people are so deceitful!

But getting back to other choice spots that you could move to, my second choice would be the south-central area of Maine near Augusta, the capital, a suburb of which is the magnificent crummy little town of Hallowell, which reflects the richness of this area with its fifteen shops on its main street that are there to sell almost exclusively to antique dealers and pickers that drive up from the rich areas around Boston, New York City and the gold coast of Connecticut.

Western Massachusetts is another top place to move to, especially because it is near the marketing areas of both the endless Boston suburbs and the Connecticut gold coast. And there is a really great year-round auction house in South Deerfield where you can fill up your station wagon any weekend and come close to doubling your money in a week selling the stuff to dealers in Connecticut and around Boston. When the "summah" people aren't around, this is one of the hottest dealers' auctions in the country. There's an auctioneers' school there, too, in case doubling your money every sixty days isn't enough for you, and you want to become a millionaire. Both are at the DOUGLAS GALLERIES.

And western Pennsylvania is one of the best buying areas of all, except that it is so far from the prime buying areas of eastern Connecticut and around Boston.

The trouble with southern Ohio is that the antiques it is rich in are strongly on the Victorian side—Ohio having been settled later than the Eastern states—and the truth is that, except for Belter furniture and Tiffany lamps, which you won't find out there anyway, there just isn't that much money in Victorian stuff these days. I know that a few years ago "Golden Oak" was getting a lot of publicity in the slick house and home magazines out of New York City. But it turned out that the only people you could sell it to were the art directors of those slick house and home magazines.

Finally, I realize that I have put the Province of Quebec on our little map but haven't mentioned it so far in this chapter. The story here is that the farmlands of southeastern Quebec—called "the Eastern Townships" by Canadians—are a treasure trove of primitive pine farmhouse furniture. Especially dough boxes, drop-leaf tables, chests of drawers and cupboards—some of which are even covered with that chalky powder-blue paint.

And for your convenience the pickers of the whole area bring them to one small town called Defoy. Here they are stored in truly vast sheds to which American pickers come and line up their trucks early in the morning to be filled up.

And, of course, you can sell this stuff back in the United States for far more than you pay for it. And getting it across the border is no problem, as antiques are not subject to duty, which is 17 percent on other things brought into the United States for resale, including reproductions like the duck and geese decoys that come in by the thousands from another little town near Defoy.

But the trouble with buying in Canada is that you are basically going into the trucking business.

However, if you still want to go there, I'll give you the directions in the chapter entitled "The Canadian Connection." You'll love looking for treasures in those vast sheds.

With my now not-so-secret map, you should be able to find your way to the antiques mother lode. Of course, there are antiques in just about every section of the country, as there has been a lot of buying and selling over the years and a lot of North-to-South and East-to-West flow of the stuff. And, as I point out further along, there are good wholesalers and regional auction houses sprinkled throughout this land of ours. Nevertheless, if you really want to strike antique gold, you are more likely to find it in the area I've sketched out on my one-of-a-kind antiques treasure hunter's map. Good hunting!

Where Anyone Can Buy at Wholesale

From one piece to a truckload

If you think that a nice little Mom and Pop antique shop on a country road is what the antiques business is all about, then you are in for another think. Because all of those shops put together are only the tip of the iceberg.

The real market for antiques is based on the fact that rich people don't buy their furniture and decorative accessories at furniture stores and shopping mall discount houses. They furnish and decorate their houses—their twenty-two-room houses—with antiques. We are talking about 5 percent of the population of the United States, which is around 12 million people, that live in houses that contain an average of three rooms per person, including children. This adds up to 36 million rooms! And supplying that market is a multibillion-dollar business.

To serve a business of that size, you obviously need wholesalers and importers to serve the interior decorators who, in turn, sell home furnishings to the very rich. That is, if *you* aren't the one who is providing those decorators with the things the very rich want.

All that English, French and Italian furniture that the interior decorators buy to sell to their clients comes into the United States by the container load through the ports of Galveston, New Orleans (and up the Mississippi), Philadelphia, New York and Boston. Some of these container loads go directly to dealers, who can order them by phone once they have established a relationship with an exporter.

Want to try a $10,000 or $20,000 container load? And don't worry about getting your money's worth—they want you to come back for more. Just write a note on your letterhead to BRITISH ANTIQUE EXPORTERS, LTD., of Newhaven, Sussex, England.

As an old advertising man myself, I'm reluctant to quote anybody's advertising on the basis that it is obviously going to be self-serving. But these Brits have a flavor all their own that I can't resist sharing with you. So here is some really convincing copy from an ad recently put out by the above-mentioned company. (And it explains how the operation works.)

> There are a great many antique shippers in Britain, but few, if any, who are as quality conscious as Norman Lefton, Managing Director of British Antique Exporters, Ltd. Fourteen years of experience shipping antiques to all parts of the globe [a lot go to Australia] have confirmed his original belief that the way to build clients' confidence is to supply them only with goods that are in first-class salable condition. To this end, he employs a full-time staff of over forty, from highly skilled packers, joiners, cabinetmak-

ers, polishers and restorers to representative buyers and executives.

Through their knowledgeable hands pass each piece of furniture before it leaves B.A.E. warehouses, assuring that the overseas buyer will only receive the best and most salable merchandise for his particular market. This attention to detail is obvious on a visit to the Newhaven warehouse, where potential customers can view what must be the most varied assortment of Georgian, Victorian, Edwardian and 1930s furniture in the area. One cannot fail to be impressed by not only the varied range of the merchandise, but by the fact that each piece is in perfect condition awaiting shipment.

As might be expected, packing is considered an art at B.A.E., and David Gilbert, the factory manager, ensures that each piece will reach its final destination in the condition a customer would wish. As a further means of improving each container load, Mr. Gilbert asks each customer to return detailed information on the salability of each piece in the container, thereby ensuring successful future shipments.

This feedback of information is the all-important factor which guarantees the profitability of future containers.

"By this method," Mr. Lefton explains, "we have established that an average £66,000 container will immediately, after it is unpacked at its final destination, realize in the region of £9,000 to £12,000 for our clients selling the goods on a quick-wholesale-turnover basis.

"These figures are confirmed by our Chartered Accountant, Mr. A. E. C. Wheeler, who whilst the official Company Accountant, is also very involved in promoting good customer relationships, and could be called our public relations genius. He is always ready to discuss the financial aspects of the shipments and proves a valued member of this highly successful company."

One of Mr. Lefton's obviously satisfied customers—and maybe his biggest, for all I know—is Morton Goldberg, who is the presiding "genius" at MORTON'S AUCTION EXCHANGE down on Magazine Street in New Orleans, where he is kept smart by his son, David Goldberg, the scholar. They are both full of the social skills that it takes to run a business that everybody can have fun at. Morton is living proof of the thesis of this book. He started his business with a few thousand dollars thirty years ago—and look at him now!

When you drive up to Morton's, it is awesome. They have two city blocks of three- and four-story warehouses full of antiques—a couple of thousand chairs here, a couple of thousand tables there, a hall full of Oriental rugs. But, of course, they can't double their money every sixty days operating on such a large scale—just once a year. Oy. I should be so poor!

But don't let that scare you. Once inside the ground floor showroom, you will feel at home. Just start looking around at the treasures, and nobody will bother you. But if you ask someone a question, they will be polite and tell you the price of anything. And please don't embarrass me by asking them if they "can do any better." You can buy one piece or, if you have brought your truck, they will escort you around to pick out the pieces you want to fill it with. They are just there to do business as nice as pecan pie. And there is an auction every week, too, which is particularly interesting to dealers and interior decorators from Southern states. Morton's is the leading auctioneering firm for the great Louisiana estates when they come on the market.

In addition to Morton's, there are three other major wholesalers scattered across the United States—Clements in Dallas, Texas, and in Chattanooga, Tennessee, and Boone's in Wilson, North Carolina. And the Beaudoins' in Canada's Province of Quebec. All these places are shockingly enormous. Morton's in New Orleans, as I've pointed out, is the equivalent of about four football fields and crammed with antiques that are used in interior decoration.

And the way you do business with them is, you just walk in and start looking around. If anybody happens to notice you, they may nod to you in a friendly way. When you find something you were looking for, you find the central desk and ask for a price on it. If it was numbered, he will look it up in a book. If not, he will go with you to look at it and give you *the* price. And there is no haggling to be done about it, because vast experience has taught these people exactly what everything is worth, and they will sell it to you at a standard 50 percent off retail value, no more no less, because they want you back to buy again—whoever you are.

Then you pay in cash or by MasterCard or Visa.

Then they load your station wagon or truck and off you go. That's all there is to it. Business is business and money is money to these people. Old customers get to pay by check or open deposit accounts, but there is no snobbery about selling to the little guy. Big oaks from little acorns grow, and they know it.

Clements of Texas, another family-operated operation of grandiose size, is on Route 20 a few miles east of Dallas. That's in Texas. But the Clements family also have a branch in Chattanooga, Tennessee—which is also gigantic in its own right.

At CLEMENTS ANTIQUES OF TEXAS, "Dallas Daddy" Charles W. Clements reigns over vast metal storage buildings crammed with the kind of ornate European antiques he imports by the container load from France, Italy and some from England to satisfy the taste of all those Texas millionaires and a few southern Californians. As with all these places, the trucks from surrounding cities line up in the morning, and every couple of weeks there is an auction for dealers—not that anyone isn't welcome if he has money to spend. And if you don't, don't go, because no junk is sold at these places.

Clements serves the whole Southwest interior decoration industry, including southern California, and the ornate style of the stock certainly shows the difference between life-styles of the East and West Coasts. The basic preferences around the United States are: English and Early American variations of it in the Northeast. American-style Empire in the South. Real French stuff of all periods around New Orleans. Used furniture in the Midwest. (Really appalling stuff!) And anything overdecorated, vulgar and pretentious in the Southwest.

CLEMENTS ANTIQUES OF CHATTANOOGA serves the Midwest and anybody on the East Coast that may be interested. Here the emphasis is on the best of English and Victorian furniture and objects—but a little bit of everything. Weekly sales and big wholesale warehouses.

Between the Chattanooga operation and Clements of Texas, Charlie flies back and forth all the time, stopping only to order container loads from Europe by telephone—like $30,000 container loads.

You will find the same thing at Boone's in Wilson, North Carolina. Not to be confused with WILSON'S in Boone, North Carolina, but it's pretty hard not to.

BOONE'S ANTIQUES is on Route 301, just south of Wilson, North Carolina. Although Edgar Boone doesn't advertise much, his business is known to every interior decorator in the country, and his warehouses are enormous. They have to be to contain the container loads of furniture and decorative accessories that he imports from England, Scotland, France, Spain and Italy. Nobody is going to insult you there, but retail trade isn't their bag and you see more trucks than vans and station wagons lined up there for loading. Rich gilded Italian and French pieces far outnumber the English classical things, and decorators come to Boone's from all over the country knowing just what to expect.

And finally we have that wonderful place in Canada that dealers have been trying to keep a secret for years. The basis for the secrecy is that if one dealer in an area in the Northeast knows about it, he doesn't want to tip off his competition. This is the BEAUDOIN BROTHERS in Defoy, Quebec. If you are looking for country pine and farmhouse furniture, and all the oil lamps, carriages, frames, spinning wheels, chests of drawers piled three high down in long narrow aisles, this is the place to be. Next to aisles of cupboards and dry sinks, and dough boxes and cobblers' benches are diamond-carved panels and snowshoe furniture for the Canadians.

Everything is unfinished and in the rough, of course, but at prices to knock your hat off.

Now while there you will sooner or later run into a chicken coop full of life-sized wooden geese in about three positions, and they are terrific for painting or just staining brown and wiping on a black glaze. But if you ask one of the *frères* where they came from, he won't have the faintest idea.

Which is a little odd, since they come from a furniture factory about two miles away, where the workers fill slack time by hand-carving them. Also ducks, rabbits and many other small animals—all selling, of course, for even less than at the *frères* Beaudoin. Last time I went there it was with the infamous Joe Patrick, who filled his station wagon with them. Fast sellers!

The location of that factory is on the same road the Beaudoin sheds are, about an equal distance on the other side of the superhighway.

If you are really paying attention, this means that there are no significant wholesalers in the Northeast, the upper Midwest or the Deep South. And the reason for this brings us back to one of the most important facts about making money in the antiques business. Antiques come from the oldest parts of the country, and there is a lot of money to be made by moving them from the old parts to the new parts. Especially from New England, New York, Pennsylvania and Virginia to that vast intellectual wasteland that is the rest of the country, where the people thirst for culture and for objects that have roots. So the wholesalers are strategically located in the hearts of the wastelands to satisfy the lust for antiques in places like Cincinnati and Dubuque. And since there isn't enough American stuff to go around in the civilized parts of the country, the imported European objects have to fill the need.

Of course, some American objects slip out of the Northeast—like the $20 oxbows that sell in Texas for $400. And don't tell me Texans aren't that dumb. I've been there and I know. Everybody wants to claim he has the oxbow with which his great granddaddy drove across the plains.

It's knowing things like that that will help you to quadruple your money in antiques in about *three* days.

If you are really serious in making a profit in this weird business, you owe it to yourself to visit one, or all, of these fabulous wholesalers, even if it's to prove to yourself that I'm not spinning one of my wild stories.

How to Buy at Auctions

And where to find the ones that sell things cheap

The first thing you have to know about auctions is that they are held all over the country at all times of the year. At least a thousand auction houses in this country hold one or more every weekend. And another two or three thousand are held during the week to liquidate estates. All you have to do to find them is to look in the classified section of any daily newspaper. Or in the three trade journals of the antiques business: *The Antiques Trader Weekly, The Antiques and Arts Weekly* and *The Maine Antique Digest.*

The largest of these tabloid size newspapers is *The Antiques Trader Weekly* with a circulation of 60,000, and it covers the Midwest like a blanket. Nobody holds an auction in the Midwest without advertising in it. Almost all of the stuff shown in the illustrated auction ads is Victorian, of course, because that's what they have there.

The second in size is confusingly called by antiques persons *The Newtown Bee.* It started out as a department in a weekly newspaper by that name and the name stuck. But it is now a big fat gold mine of information called *The Antiques and Arts Weekly*, published by the Bee Publishing Co., Newtown, Connecticut 06470. It costs about $12.50 for six months, and it blankets the Northeast. It is the *essential* trade journal of the Wonderful World of Antiques. In this paper the auction ads show the best of the international marketplace for antiques: English, French and American, Chinese, Persian and whatever. It is edited by R. Scudder Smith, which has nothing to do with anything, except that I can't leave out such a wonderful name.

Another great name is that of Samuel Pennington, who is the editor of *The Maine Antique Digest.* This tabloid trade journal, whose address is Box 358, Waldoboro, Maine 04572, covers the Americana marketplace, which is rich and thriving, bustling with announcements of upcoming auctions—in spite of those dumb antique dealers with negative personalities who are always whining that they can't find any antiques any more.

So to find the auctions, you follow the trade journals and your daily newspaper. In other parts of this book, I've established the things you should buy and the things you shouldn't touch with an eleven-foot pole. But there still remain a few matters of technique of how to handle yourself at auctions that you should consider.

The first thing is that only a person with a trust fund would bid at an auction unless he or she has been to the preview of the auction to inspect the merchandise for flaws and to pick out the pieces he or she is going to bid on, forsaking all others no matter how cheaply they seem to be selling for.

These previews are held during a couple of hours before the auction begins. Or for some big auctions the day before, usually in the afternoon.

When it comes time for the auction, grab yourself a seat right up front where the auctioneer can see you, and get him to like you. Auctioneers are not machines, and even if they try to be fair they can't help from time to time, for whatever their reasons, but show preference by closing easily on a bid and not pushing for another bid over it.

But, you say, how could I possibly get the auctioneer to like me with all those other people out there for him to like? Why should he particularly turn on to me if I am a short dumpy old lady and a lousy dresser who is sitting behind a row of young fashion models who are friends of his daughter who has brought them to see her father's auction?

It's easy.

All you have to do is think in terms of what the auctioneer wants out of life. Or which of his needs can you fulfill, as we say at the Grotz Psychoanalytic Institute. The answer is obvious. He needs somebody to start the bidding. Not on everything, but some things. And when these moments come up, you come to his rescue.

So the first two rules for buying at an auction are: you do your homework at the preview, and you seduce the auctioneer.

The next problem is to know how much to bid on the items you've singled out—all from our list of the fastest sellers, of course. And that is easy, too. Even if you are a complete beginner and know practically nothing about the comparative value of antiques.

The secret to this is understanding—or accepting—that all bids you make at an auction are made *against* someone else's bid. Therefore, you never bid against a civilian—as opposed to a dealer. This is because a civilian can have all kinds of sentimental or emotional reasons for wanting an object. He also may be, as Ron Barlow says, "drunk or in love."

On the other hand, the dealers who are bidding at the auction—if they have survived in the business very long—will be realists. And, assuming that they aren't in the dumb dealer class, they'll be realists who know values and they will have decided in advance on price ranges (usually low) that they will pay for the objects they want.

Thus you are always safe in bidding a little bit over a dealer. And after you have done this a couple of times, he will sense when you are after an object and tend to drop out early and let you have it—especially if you demonstrate that you will do the same for him.

Incidentally, it is easy to tell the dealers from the civilians, because the dealers are all in the front row. As you should be. So as a general rule, you never bid against a voice that comes from behind you.

And of course you smile a lot at the dealers in the front row to indicate that you will cooperate with them in any piracy they may want to commit. The sign that they are looking for your cooperation—to return to you on future objects—is when they bid quickly and fairly high on something that comes up. You smile at them—they will be watching you—and pointedly don't bid at all.

The logical extension of this is called "the dealer's ring," which may be made up of a long-established gang of outlaws, but is usually quite casually formed at the preview.

Whenever you recognize a dealer at a preview, you smile pleasantly at him or her and say, "Aren't these things commonplace (or ugly)? But I sure would like to have that piece over there." Five will get you ten that that dealer's face will light up and he or she will come back with, "Oh, I particularly like this piece over here." This is not whispered but done as loudly as possible so that any other cooperation-seekers can hear and get in on the act, too. Oh, how easily a ring is formed when pirates meet on common ground!

You'll be surprised by just how quickly you'll get the hang of buying at auctions. Just know what you are buying, the top price you will pay, the people you are bidding against and butter up to the auctioneer.

So now let us say that by going to one good auction or two average ones, you have gotten the hang of things and have managed to put $1,000 worth of our fastest-moving antiques into the back of your station

wagon—or the trunk of your old car if you haven't bought any furniture. Now where do you take them?

Well, you sure don't take them home and put them in your barn or shop like all those dumb antique dealers out there do. You leave them right in that car, and you sell them out of that car.

Where? To whom? And for how much?

Read on, Macduff!

The Great Regional Auction Houses

That are combined with giant wholesale warehouses where you can fill up your truck at 60 percent off retail any day of the week—and without ever being cheated, either

Now the fact is, that every dealer you ever meet will tell you about his secret sources back in the woods of wherever you are. Or about the old ladies in the old-age home whose friendship he has cultivated for many years who are now feeding him their best pieces one at a time. Or the friend he has at the big-city storage company who tips him off whenever one of the storage rooms gets behind in its payments and the storage company is ready to sell the contents of the vault just for the delinquent rent.

But the simple truth of the matter is that 99.99 percent of all antiques you will ever see in an antique shop were either bought by the dealer at an auction or by a picker who bought it at an auction and sold it to the dealer for a small profit—thus doubling his money in ninety days or less, of course.

That's just the way it works, folks. And there are

hundreds of pickers out there doubling their money in *thirty* days or less buying at auctions and selling to dealers. I just put sixty days in the title of this book because I was afraid of scaring you off by sounding too much like a con man. And a little bit because when you are just starting, it *may* take you sixty days —if you are lazy.

Getting on with it, there are probably around 15,000 good auction houses in the country. They are in every big city, middle city and little city. Some are in small towns and even out in the middle of nowhere because somebody bought an old cow-barn cheap in which to hold the winter auctions of the "contents" of people who just happen to die in the winter.

And the way to find them is to look in your local newspaper. In the bigger cities you look in the Friday edition, because most auctions are held on Saturdays. And off you drive in your van or station wagon with a few hundred dollars to start learning the hard way—but also to have a lot of fun and meet a whole bunch of other people also having a lot of fun doing the same thing you are.

But everybody always wants to know about the BIG auction houses where the dealers go to buy—not just at the weekly auctions, but in the wholesale barns that usually go with these big auction houses devoted to serving the trade.

So here is a list of them, and since they are all a little bit different there is no logical way to put them in order except alphabetically. And they are spread all around the country. From northern New York to New Orleans to Texas to Tennessee to Virginia and

North Carolina to Ohio and up to Maine. So, alphabetically, they are:

BONNER'S BARN, Malone, New York—To get there you have to find Albany, which is the capital of the state, and drive straight north on a fine superhighway until you are almost to Canada. About ten miles from Canada you turn left and in about fifteen minutes you will come to the little city of Malone, which looks like it was left over from around 1922—a good set for a gangster movie. Bonner's barn is on the street next to the Post Office on the top of the hill in the center of town. The twenty-fifth house—with the big barn in back.

This place specializes in the best of Americana—the weathervanes without bullet holes in them, whirligigs and furniture with the original paint or decoration on it. And the best things that Bob Bonner and his wife Jamie keep inside their house could just as well be on display in the Museum of American Folk Art. Fantastic—and all for sale. Except for the dining room table and a few other basic pieces, of course, but Jamie still has to keep her eye on them, ever since Bob sold her sewing table one day when she was out to the store.

GARTH'S AUCTION BARN is located just outside of Delaware, Ohio, which is in the south-central part of the state about thirty miles north of Columbus, Ohio.

This is one of the few major sources of antiques that does not include a wholesale barn. But it does hold weekly auctions of both routine, general-stock antiques and almost weekly auctions of fine estates that attract dealers from as far as Minnesota, wherever that is.

By "fine estates," I mean the best of Middle American antiques. Which is to say they are certainly equal in character to the antiques of New England, but they tend to be more really American as a group. You will find far fewer pieces of the English furniture styles that were so widely copied along the Eastern seaboard from Boston to Philadelphia. I suppose what I am trying to say is that you could characterize the objects that pass through Garth's as the finest of American farm-country antiques. And the prices are considerably lower for similar pieces, even those at Eastern dealers' auctions. Another gold mine for the quick-turnover dealer and picker who wants to double his money in sixty days or less.

JULIA'S ANTIQUES—This operation of auctions and wholesale selling is not run by "Aunt Julia," but by canny James D. Julia, and has the advantage of being smack in the middle of Maine antique country, which is to say on Route 201 just north of Fairfield—about 150 miles north of Portland. He offers good, low prices—maybe the lowest around—on a wide variety of merchandise.

The WILSON GALLERIES—This famous auction house is located in the middle of Virginia at a wide spot in the road called Verona. Thus the father-and-son team that run this business are naturally known as the "two gentlemen from Verona." Here you will find all the best of Southern and horse-country antique furniture and decorative plantation objects being auctioned from a giant turntable in the middle of an amphitheater originally built for auctioning fine horses and livestock. (It's like going to the movies!)

I've told you in another chapter about these gigantic wholesale operations, such as Clements Antiques of Dallas and Chattanooga and Boone's Antiques of Wilson, North Carolina. They do a by-truckload business but they also hold weekly sales where you can pick up those one, two or three good items that you are looking for.

As you gain more experience, the dealers you do business with will, in the course of their conversation, tip you off to all the other good regional auction houses that are out there. Just bring money!

Some People Are So Deceitful

Or, ripping off charity stores for fun and profit

I once knew a very successful antique dealer who operated out of some barns on the edge of a middle-sized city in the Northeastern section of our republic. And he developed a wonderful source for his business. He found a used furniture store operated by a local charity group. So he started by stopping by the store every morning to see if any new antiques had passed through the restoration rooms and been put out on the floor of the store.

Well, pretty soon he managed to make friends with a saleslady there and was quite open with her about the fact that he was trying to get to any new antiques before someone else got them, as they are notoriously misunderstood and therefore often insanely underpriced.

That's all he had to do. He just had to pay attention to somebody, a lady who was no longer young and beautiful and needed somebody to pay attention to her. In no time at all *she* suggested that if anything came in during the afternoon she could call him on the telephone to come on down before any of the other dealers who also visited the store regularly could get a chance to see it.

Ha! The way I tell the story makes them sound like a couple of nice old folks helping each other. The crooks.

But after a while even this wasn't good enough for this fellow. Sometimes he had to pay up to half as much as the objects were worth. Why, once he had to pay a whole $150 for a *real* Governor Winthrop slant-front desk that some rich old lady had donated to the charity.

So one day he called up the store and asked to have their truck sent to his house because he had some old furniture to donate that their handicapped workers could fix up for sale in their store.

When the two old reformed derelicts who drove the truck arrived, he treated them like princes. In fact, he got them drunk in his living room so he could show them the kinds of things he was looking for to *buy*. And when they left, he handed them each an extra pint of pretty good whiskey.

Well, you just know that the next time they made a collection run they stopped by their generous friend's house before they returned to the store.

And from then on my friend didn't give them whiskey anymore, just $5 each (this was thirty years ago) and picked out the best piece or two in the truck. They even carried the loot into one of his barns for him.

Ain't it a shame. Some people are so deceitful.

How to Sell the Things You Buy

Or, the gentle art of getting your buyers to work for you

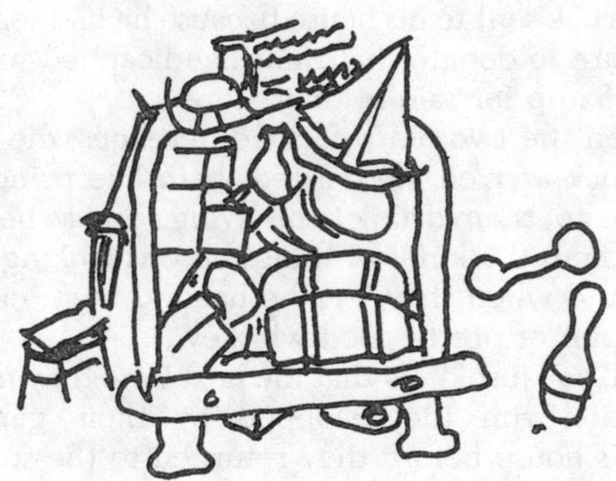

All right. Let's say you have believed everything that I have told you so far. You have found one of the low-priced, dealer-oriented auction houses and have invested your $500 or $600 to fill up your van or old station wagon with some of the quick-turnover objects of the current market in antiques. Now what are you going to do? Where are you going to go to sell your stock?

Well, of course, unless you are a ninny, you have thought this over in advance, and you know exactly where you are going. And what you have thought over is that every decent-sized city in the country has its wealthy suburb or suburbs, and in them you are going to find the interior decorators where the better-off of us get our rooms furnished with antiques. And a little farther out in the country from the suburbs you are going to find some antique shops scattered around.

And just for your convenience these shops will have joined in a loose association that puts out a folder telling about the various shops and including a map of how to find them. And if these shops are to stay in business, they need a constant flow of merchandise—which is exactly what you have to offer them. As long as you and they can come to a reasonable agreement about how much your merchandise is worth.

And as a beginner you are naturally unsure about values, and you are afraid of not getting enough. Well, there are a lot of things about this to consider that will make you feel better.

The first is that any sane dealer is glad to see you and look at your stuff. He needs you, and he needs you to come back. In fact, all the dealers I know practically force themselves to buy at least one piece just to get you to come back. It's just a reasonable policy on their part.

The second thing is that you should think of calling on a dealer as a learning experience. You are now going to college in antiques. Any dealer will be perfectly glad to talk to you about why anything is worth something or not. After all, the dealer wants you to know what to look for to be out there buying for him.

Another thing is to try to remember that you are not trying to get rich in one day—you've got fifty-nine left to go. So as a rule of thumb, you should just ask him to pay you 20 percent more than you paid for each of your objects. If he doesn't buy at your price, smile, wish him good luck and go on to the next dealer. If he also shakes his head negatively at this price—and that's all he'll do, he won't offer you less—smile, wish him good luck and go about your rounds. When you come to the third dealer who appears interested in the item, offer it to him for exactly what you paid for it *and get your money back so you can invest it more wisely tomorrow.* In fact, if you have made a bad mistake in what you paid for the object, you'll just have to take a loss, and you should take it as fast as you can so you can stop wasting time and space on a loser. Besides, you'll be getting back at least some of your money to use again.

And then, before you say good-bye to the dealer, go into the heart of any successful business: research and development. Meaning, of course, that you ask the dealer what he would like you to bring him the next time you come by. And he will tell you. Because getting you to bring him what he wants is an essential part of his business. And you are now learning things faster than you have ever learned anything before. Because it is your money and your greed for more of it that are the pieces in the wonderful game of antiques that you are now playing. And it's fun, and you are not working for anybody else, even if you are only doing it part-time. And you are looking forward to coming back to that dealer, and he is looking forward to seeing you again. Man, you're needed. You are part of the real world.

And now the most important part of all: your little black book. In this you write down the name and address of the dealer and make some notes about what he told you he was looking for. And most important of all his telephone number! Because the most important thing you can do is to call a dealer on the telephone to inquire about a piece you have seen—perhaps at an auction preview—that is on his wanted list. And this isn't just an intelligent procedure. It is SELLING. Because the first principle in selling is to involve the customer in a decision-making process. Which is worlds away from a buy-or-not-buy process.

Long ago when I sold typewriters for Remington Rand, the first thing I learned was that you *never* ask a person to buy your typewriter. What you do is you bring two typewriters with you, and you demonstrate the different features of both. Then when you have gotten him interested in comparing the differences between the two of them, you whip out your order book and say, "Which one do you like best?" And when this poor fellow makes up his mind, you push your order book in front of him to sign his name before he knows what has happened to him. Oh, some people are so deceitful.

Getting back to your telephone call to the dealer. Let's say the piece you have spotted is a slant-front desk. Sometimes called a Governor Winthrop desk. Not a great 200-year-old one worth $10,000–$30,000, but a good reproduction made by some furniture company in the 1920s or 1930s. Not really an antique, but a very desirable object that very often moves through the antiques business.

So you describe the desk to the dealer in detail. And he will ask you questions about it—which will educate you some more. And he will tell you what it is worth to him, if the two of you have communicated well. So you now know how much you can afford to pay for it or bid on it if it is going at auction. Free education. *And* you have the dealer working in your purchasing department for free, too.

So you don't bid more than 80 percent of what the dealer has tentatively agreed to pay you, if you have communicated well. And even if he does back out of the deal, you know you have made a reasonable investment for a possible sale to another dealer.

And what if you get the desk for only half of what you were willing to pay for it? Aha! Now that's the Joy of Antiques, for sure. Are you going to tell the dealer that? And sell the desk to him for only 20 percent more than you paid for it? I doubt it. Oh, some of you people are so deceitful!

But it's fun, isn't it?

So the final line is that you have to build up working relationships with a string of dealers. Then you take your purchases to them, buying at the auctions that take place on the weekends and going around to your dealers during the week. Or, of course, you can do the same thing part-time or, if you are old like me, just in the warm weather. It's nice out there in the summah!

How to Pay for Your Winter Vacation in Florida Buying and Selling Antiques

Pay for your Florida vacation by buying and selling antiques? I know it sounds crazy, but it's true! Who ever thinks of Florida as having any antiques in it? The state's just filled with plastic woven chairs and shiny stainless steel bar stools; at least that's what we think. But that is because we are not as smart as my friend Harry the Shark, who told me all about this. Well, at least we don't think the same way Harry does.

The secret is that there *are* plenty of antiques in Florida. And they are selling every winter at far lower prices than you can sell them for when you bring them back up North with you when your vacation is over.

The premise, of course, is that you travel down and back in an old station wagon. What Harry actually does is send his wife and kids back by night plane so he can stuff his wagon really full. Harry makes enough on his deals not only to cover the airfare expenses but also to put his family up in a cottage for two weeks. Obviously Harry's maneuver can be carried out on a smaller scale or even by renting a U-Haul one way from Florida northward.

Where do they come from, these antiques that Harry buys? Well, it's a little grim, but what happens is that thousands and thousands of couples that grow old up North retire to a nice little house in Florida for their old age. And the ones who had furnished their houses with antiques over the years bring South with them a few of *their best pieces* to remind them of the good old days.

And then after a while they die. I'm sorry, but that's just the way life goes. I hope they die happy and don't suffer. But that is not really our concern. By their very nature, all antiques once belonged to somebody who now is dead. And Harry, of course, has never even thought of this aspect of antiques. Like all good antique operators, he is a sound, practical, profoundly insensitive man. When I brought this up to him, "Sensitive," he says, "that's a loser, isn't it?"

So now what happens to such antiques? Why they go on sale at a local auction house, of course, to settle the estate. The old folks' children are running computers and raising kids in a suburb of Minneapolis. What do they care about antiques. "Just send the money," they write the bank. At least, that's the way it happens the majority of the times.

So off to the auction houses around Miami and St. Petersburg the antiques go, and who goes to those auctions? Old people, of course, with nothing else to do. And they already have more of their own antiques stuffed into their little retirement homes than they have space for.

The result is that the average going prices at these auctions is half the price the same pieces bring at gallery auctions in Cleveland or Pittsburgh or Rutland, or wherever. There is no problem about whether you can double your money or not. The only problem is how much better you can do by buying only the kinds of objects that are fast resellers when you get back up North.

Incidentally, in case you are totally naive, the way you find the auction houses in Florida is by looking in the Friday newspapers for the ads the big auction houses run every week for their Saturday—and other day—auctions. As to what to buy and how to do it, that's all in other chapters of this book.

And one last piece of advice. You have probably heard about some famous antiques town on the east coast of Florida that is full of hundreds of shops full of wonderful antiques. Well, I hate to have to be the one to disillusion you, but the only town like that is Hallowell, Maine, mentioned earlier, which is about two thousand miles due north.

There is a town on the east coast of Florida, all right, and it's called Delray Beach, which is a nice warm place to live or spend the winter. But the eight antique shops there contain the worst collection of unsalable, unwanted, dingy, dark-brown objects ever assembled on the face of the earth. You won't find any of the fastest selling antiques in any of these shops, and you can't find any of them in Delray Beach. Or if on the wild chance that you do find one or two, they will be fantastically overpriced, because everything there is. This is sucker town for tourists who can be conned into thinking that an antique is something that is dirty, old and useless. So obviously my friend Harry wouldn't be caught dead in Delray. Of course, he helped me to write our chapter on the factors that make a fast-selling antique.

As to Hallowell, Maine, it's right outside the capital of Maine, which is Augusta, and that's a halfway stop on your summer trip up to the big secret antiques "dump" in Canada, but I told you all about those places in the chapter on wholesale sources.

And since some cynic in the back row is sure to ask if I ever paid for my vacation in Florida this way, the answer is yes. And it was a lot of fun, too. As for you, just know what to buy, and you can do it, too!

The Canadian Connection

An almost secret wholesaler of country antiques

The little town of Defoy, which I've already mentioned a few times, is one of the most secret places in the world. For two reasons. The first is that you can't find it on an American road map. And I mean those American road maps that show the southern part of the Province of Quebec where the town is located. That, I suppose, is because somebody decided it was too small.

The second is that if you know about a gold mine where you can buy all the old pine cupboards you want for $35 a piece, you don't go around telling everybody you know how to find the place. One young antique dealer is said to have married an ugly old woman to find out where it was. And all you had to do was buy this book. What a bargain!

The best way to get there—with your big old empty station wagon, of course—is to take Route 3 up through New Hampshire. When you get to the border crossing, don't bother asking the guards where Defoy is. They might know, but being French, they won't tell you. All Frenchmen—even French Canadians—hate all foreigners. Just jealous, I guess.

Then head north to Montreal on a surprisingly little-traveled country road without any gas stations—for which contingency you have already filled your tank south of the border down America way.

At a Montreal gas station you can get a map that shows Defoy. It is just off of a nifty scenic superhighway that runs northeast from Montreal to Quebec City. It is on the right side of the highway about three fifths of the way from Montreal to Quebec City. There is just one little sign out in the middle of nowhere, so don't miss it.

Defoy is only about a mile from the highway. On the way you will pass what is undoubtedly the worst restaurant in the Northern hemisphere. Don't stop there. The food they throw on the counter in front of you—no plates—is beyond description. Then you will come to the town, which consists of only a dozen or so houses scattered around what looks like a junkyard, operated, a large sign declares, by H. BEAUDOIN ET FRÈRES. And if you get there on a nice spring morning there will be eight or ten trucks lined up in front of the yard waiting their turn to get loaded up from the enormous tin sheds of the brothers Beaudoin.

In these sheds you can walk down 400-foot-long aisles between chests of drawers stacked four high. Trunks stacked six high, *et cetera, et cetera.* There is a room that must have three thousand oil lamps in it. Tons of china. Fifty or sixty buggies. All at prices so low you would feel like a creep to argue about them. Not that you would get anywhere, of course.

And it is an interesting story of where it all came from. Or rather, why it came there. What happened is that the Eastern Townships of the Province of Quebec used to be the breadbasket of the eastern half of Canada—vast fertile farmlands divided up into twenty or thirty thousand family farms. But with the advances made in modern farm machinery these farms gradually have become too small to make a living on, and they are either being consolidated into bigger farms or sold as summer homes to the rich people from Montreal. So when the old houses were razed to make bigger fields or cleaned out for resale to the rich people, their contents were trucked up to Defoy for some quick cash. Not much, but quick.

Of course all those farms also had buggies. And these are lined up in a field behind the tin barns of Beaudoin. The last time that I was up there watching the trucks and station wagons from the United States get loaded with pine cupboards, there was one fellow there with an old tractor trailer of the type used to deliver new cars to automobile dealers. And onto this rig he had stacked or fitted fourteen buggies, mostly of the family size with the fringe on top.

So what did he want them for? The best I could come up with was that he could sell them to nurserymen to make planters out of them to put in millionaires' front yards. But that didn't seem like a hot market, so I asked him why he liked buggies so much. And he told me. He said he came from Pennsylvania, and they sold like hot cakes to the Amish people down in Lancaster County. He said he just drove around from farm to farm and would sell all fourteen in three or four days. He had picked out the ones in best condition that had been sitting unused in barns for the last fifty years, so the Amish could start going to church in them right away if their own buggies had worn out.

I also wormed it out of him that he paid an average of just under $100 a piece for them and sold them for around $400. So even after expenses of, say, $1,400 for maintaining and running his truck, he made a profit of $200 on each buggy. So *he* had found a way to double his money in antiques in *two weeks!*

As to the other people who buy at Defoy, they are called "pickers"—that is, people who buy at these low prices for quick resale to antique dealers who have shops. And what they do is buy the most expensive things they can find in relationship to bulk, which is to say the amount of space they are going to take up in their station wagon or truck. And of course they know the kinds of objects the dealers they sell to are looking for.

However, pickers who spend their lives running back and forth to Defoy seem to me to have chosen a hard row to hoe. Basically, they have gone into the truck-driving business. It probably takes them two trips to double their original investment, but what a way to live.

From the point of view of the Harvard School of Business Administration, the trouble with Defoy is that the merchandise doesn't cost enough for us to turn over enough money for the time involved. So in case you are ever in the Province of Quebec, Defoy is certainly worth a stop. Especially if you buy some of the more expensive stripped pieces of pine that they have recently started selling there.

And oh, yes. There is another advantage to a trip to Defoy. You get to visit Montreal, and Montreal has a couple of streets of the best inexpensive restaurants in the world. Mostly French restaurants, of course, but the Chinese ones with the French chefs will drive your palate out of its mind. If you have ever thought of eating yourself to death, this is the place to do it.

Fakes to Watch Out For

Unless you can check them out first with an expert in the particular field

Nobody wants to talk about fakes. Nobody wants to hear about them or read about them. And God knows I have never been able to make a nickel writing about them in over thirty-five years of trying. And I've seen a dozen books about them over the years that must have sold twenty-five or thirty copies each. All publishing disasters.

However, how can I call this a book about the antiques business without holding at least one class on the subject? So for any of you who haven't just remembered a previous appointment, here goes.

Since we all know that greed is man's purest emotion, the antiques forger has always been with us. In ancient Rome there were antique dealers selling fake statues that were supposed to have come from ancient Greece. They bought one real one and set a local boy to copying it in the back room.

But nowadays the things you have to watch out for especially are folk art, weathervanes, primitive watercolor "itinerant" portraits, primitive oil paintings and, in the furniture field, decorated six-board chests, tripod tables, Windsor chairs and the early chairs made up of turned pieces such as the "Brewster" chair. Also Tiffany-type lampshades and bases, cast-iron toys, Rembrandt etchings and English glass and china.

So herewith some random notes on things to look for or at least understand about these commonly faked antiques.

Folk Art

The world of antiques is rife with stories about painted wooden figures and farm animals that have been sold back and forth among dealers rising gradually in price from $65 to $95 to $150 and then suddenly to appear in full color in *The Magazine Antiques* at $12,000. It just isn't that hard for a craftsman or artist to mix a little raw umber into a pale blue paint to get that old milk paint patina. Then to distress the piece by beating it with some rusty old chains and then apply a tinted dull glaze. After this, using a hair dryer will complete the process by creating lots of age-old tiny crack marks. I mean *de*ceitful!

Of course, the dealers themselves are responsible for the proliferation of these fakes. After all, what is a dealer going to do when he finds out he has put out $300 or $400 for a fake? Hang a sign on it saying, FAKE? Not bloody likely. He's just going to forget he knows it's a fake and take it to Brimfield, Massachusetts, next spring to get rid of it at what he paid for it. (You can sell anything at Brimfield in the spring! See "Where to Buy Good Stuff Cheaply.") And that is what you better do too. Unless, of course, you want to take it into New York City, and sell it to one of those shops that advertise in *The Magazine Antiques.*

Copper Weathervanes

These are forged more easily than you might think at first consideration. A mold of a well-greased original—or an original wood carving—is first made with fiberglass and resin. The same kind you can buy in any boatyard. One mold for each side. Then you back these up with concrete, and using a wooden or rubber mallet, you hammer sheets of copper into the molds. It's the same copper sheet that is used for flashing and copper roofs.

The two halves are then soldered together exactly as the original ones were. A bath in the proper acid gives them an instant patina. Then the forger puts it up on the roof of his barn and waits for a rich dentist from New York City to drive by. Or he props it up in front of his antique shop, or whatever.

Watercolor Portraits

These were originally made by itinerant artists, who meandered from farm to farm back when everybody lived on a farm, and they were especially popular in the middle 1800s. And since, as any artist will tell you, a watercolor portrait is the hardest thing in art to do, they are all bad. Which makes them an absolute cinch to duplicate, even for people with virtually no artistic talent. And these "no talents" may even paint the best or "most interesting" phony pieces.

Of course you do have to kill the brightness of your

colors with a touch of their opposite on the color wheel, but that isn't real hard to learn to do.

But you have to have old paper, you say? Easy. It comes from the folio-size record books that have been kept in courthouses and other county offices practically since the country began. There is always a blank page or two in the front and back of them. And if these sheets don't look old enough, you can always bake them in your oven for a few hours. So there are lots of these around, too, and you are talking about objects worth $1,500 to $2,500. Which is the reason you hardly ever hear anything about these fakes. People have too much money invested in them to even question their authenticity, much less think about how easily they can be forged. Remember what the Greeks, or somebody, used to do with a bearer of bad news? That's why if you start talking about fakes at any gathering of antiques people, you soon find yourself standing alone in the middle of the room with a soggy martini in your hand.

Oil Paintings

The ones to watch out for here are primitives and portraits in the manner of famous portrait artists. Your newly discovered example of some old master's work is the most likely suspect. And it happens all the time. Remember the Dutch artist who faked many $100,000 Holbeins for thirty years and got away with it.

All you need is an old painting of no particular interest. They are usually the work of a student. The old paint is simply removed with paint remover so the surface will be smoother, and off you go. I have heard that the really good forgeries are currently coming out of Taiwan.

The Grandma Moses primitives are done the same way. One artist supplies a New York City store with one a month—for $1,000 a canvas. And, of course, what is known is only the tip of the iceberg.

Tiffany-Type Lampshades

Good reproductions of the colored glass shades that used to hang over dining room tables in Victorian times have been around for years.

Furniture

Antique furniture is so easy to fake that one great museum even has a room set aside to exhibit the fakes it has bought by mistake. And most of these were discovered only by X-raying the joints to discover marks made by modern tools. For instance, the marks made by circular saws, which didn't come into use until around 1890.

But those are extreme cases, and there are many fakes you can detect if you know what to look for. For instance:

Perfectly flat surfaces are a dead giveaway. They can be obtained only with a big modern planing machine or a hand-held belt sander with a four-inch-wide belt. In the old days surfaces were smoothed with scrapers that had slightly curved cutting edges so that corners of the edge wouldn't scratch the surface. As a result, you can see shallow waves on a true old surface when you hold it against the light.

Regular, machine-cut dovetails didn't appear before 1900, when the machine to make them was invented. Old dovetails are few and far between, and no two are exactly alike.

Leaves of tables that are made of two boards "joined" or glued together also cry fake, because in olden times there were plenty of big trees around to make wide boards, and they did.

Small round tabletops are also interesting, because if they are really old, they will have shrunk across the grain to make them slightly oval—at least a quarter of an inch, even on one only fifteen inches in diameter. A lot more on bigger ones. Center posts and round legs also become slightly oval, and you can detect this with an ordinary caliper. (The only trouble with this is that a really serious faker will preshrink the pieces of his fake by roasting them in an oven at three hundred degrees for three days. Oh, some people are so deceitful!)

Patina is another sign of age. It is a slight obscurity of the figure, a pale cast or smoke, caused by the top fibers of the wood drying out with the finish over a hundred years. But then, again, the real master fakers can duplicate this, too. They treat the bare wood surface with a solution of lye in water to raise the surface fibers before they apply a shellac finish. This is done before the baking, which also creates the patina effect. Oh, it's a complicated business and the fakers all keep secrets from each other, such as putting an old-looking crackle in their finishes by a method nobody will tell me. Not even Roy Simmons, and he's supposed to be my friend.

Price Guides

And the real winners were finally put out by Knopf, which genial Scudder Smith likes a lot

Everyone knows the trouble with price guides.

They give you one line of information. Such as "Cast-iron dog andiron, pair . . . $25." Well, what the heck does that tell you? They could be beautiful or ugly. What kind of a dog? A greyhound or a bulldog? Workmanship? Cleaned? Dirty? On a good day at an auction when prices were high? Or at the end of a bad auction when things were going for nothing?

One day I was talking to a young picker down at Leonard's Antiques in Seekonk, Massachusetts. It's a big place on old Route 41, a few miles east of Providence. They specialize in selling beds and other furniture to interior decorators from the Midwest. All finished stuff.

Well, this young picker had brought in a wreck of a cannon-ball post bed made of maple and cherry. But it was about 150 years old, so it was good raw material for widening and refinishing, so he was asking $100 for it and naturally was glad to settle for $65.

Well, I got to talking to him—his name was Jim—and when he found out I was a writer, he said, "Why don't you write a price guide that tells something about the thing?"

And I *heard* what he said and thought about it a long time. I even tried a few myself. But then along came the price guides to end all price guides that anybody who wants to make money in the antiques business *must* run out and buy.

These are the *Knopf Collectors' Guides to American Antiques*, published by Alfred A. Knopf, Inc. And any bookstore will order any one or all of them for you. They are printed in full color and show over three hundred representative pieces in each of eight fields of antiques. With lots and lots of descriptive copy about each piece and the market for them. Plus a really intelligent price range for each object.

These eight guides cover:

FURNITURE—chairs, tables, sofas and beds.
FURNITURE—chests, cupboards, desks and other pieces.
FOLK ART—paintings, sculpture and country objects.
POTTERY AND PORCELAIN—stoneware, redware, Rockingham, art pottery, yellow ware, sponge ware, everything.
GLASS—tableware, bowls and vases.
GLASS—bottles, lamps and other objects.
QUILTS—coverlets and rugs.
DOLLS—American, plus French and German sold in the United States.

I really can't tell you how good these things are without quoting from one of them. Just listen to this copy about a silhouette metal weathervane (which is preceded by a good color photo and a rundown on dimensions of the piece and the materials usually used):

BLOW, GABRIEL, BLOW

Comment: The Archangel Gabriel, God's messenger in the Bible, was a popular weathervane figure during the 19th century. It exists in silhouette and 3-dimensional forms made of either wood or metal. Sheet metal weathervanes were particularly common during the third quarter of the 19th century. Some were made from one piece of metal, others from three or four small pieces soldered together. When a piece became popular, dies cast from a wooden pattern, or model, were used for stamping out the components from which the figure was assembled. Finishing touches were done by hand.

Hints for Collectors: During the last several years silhouette weathervanes from Haiti have flooded the market. These vanes are cut from old oil drums, and lack the supporting braces of the antique example shown here. Thus they are merely decorative. Metal vanes are quite easy to fake, so check the provenance, and get a written guarantee of authenticity from a dealer, especially when the purchased piece is costly. [A provenance is the history of the ownership of an object.]

Now *that's* a price guide. And in the back of the book you are given a very reasonably broad price range of from $6,500 to $15,000. It's a goodie—if real. And now you know how to tell the difference between a real one and a fake.

All that the other big-selling price guides give you is a one-line listing and a price that doesn't mean anything because you have no idea of what particular piece it relates to. But the Knopf guides are something else. Let's say it takes you two days to carefully read each of the eight books. In sixteen days you will have earned yourself a Ph.D. in American antiques!

Anybody Want to Buy a Stuffed Chicken?

Always look for the unique—or sort of almost unique. The reason for this is that unique things can be worth anything you say they are, because there is nothing to compare them to on a value scale. And, of course, you are going to think low value when you are buying the object and high value when selling it.

For instance, have you ever seen a stuffed chicken? Stuffed by a taxidermist, that is? Well, in all my misspent time running around flea markets and checking out antique shops I've only seen one. It was on a nice sunny day out at the Brimfield flea market in Massachusetts where dealers go to sell to each other. And just by chance I saw that chicken. The first dealer had it for sale for $15. A few hours later I saw it for sale at another dealer's table for $35. And that afternoon I saw it—the same damned chicken—for sale for $65, and the lady dealer who had it was sure she would sell it. "Worth a hundred and twenty-five dollars," she said. "Very rare!"

Well, this is the real reason for the current boom in folk art and all the fakes of it—because each piece is unique, and dealers can get rich on it by wildly escalating its price.

That's why things like cigar store Indians, ship's figureheads and handmade weathervanes can sell from $50,000 to $100,000. Uniqueness. And the nerve to stun a farmer by offering him $1,000 for his weathervane, and once you own it to stick a $30,000 price tag on it. I know a dealer that does this—a lot—and I must say I share his glee. And there is not a dishonest thing about it, because something unique is worth whatever anybody will pay for it.

You ought to see my stuffed chicken I finally bought for only $1.25 from the fourth dealer who had it that day. What a steal! Really unique. But just because I like you, I'll let you have it for $250.

How to Stock a Parlor Shop

Getting rich in antiques is especially fun for couples. The way it works is that he goes out to do the buying, and she stays home and runs a little shop in the garage or a room in their house, which is called a "parlor shop." They both also exhibit at local antique shows and quality flea markets. It's called a mom-and-pop operation. And since most of this book is about how Pop operates in the antiques business, this chapter is about Mom's side of things.

Now, don't think I am patronizing the moms. They can be very sharp operators, indeed, and they come in all sizes and shapes and some with Southern accents that can sell you the ears off a mule to decorate your cottonwood tree. But getting back to how to stock a parlor shop, the first thing you have to do is to get rid of the idea that you have to try to sell all the junk that Pop couldn't sell to other dealers on his way home from some auction. You take all that stuff and put it in bushel baskets on your front lawn with a big "$1" sign on it. That's the advertising end of your operation and the only one worth the money it costs because it doesn't cost anything. And works better than anything else, too! Incidentally, that "$1"—or "$5" or "$22.50"—is the best headline to use for any mail-order selling you do through advertising in the antiques trade press, too, to get your ad read. Everybody has to check out an ad that just gives a price as its headline. Learned that from John Shrager, the best mail-order copywriter in the history of advertising, may his tricky soul rest in peace.

The second thing is that you want to just stock small objects so they will be easy to carry away in a car.

And the third is that the objects shouldn't be so small that they will fit in a handbag—for the obvious reason. Though, of course, if you go into jewelry, you can get some glass cases that open only from the back.

And now for the really important principle—you don't stock anything that retails for less than $10, and mostly from $20 up. That's because if you sell ten $1 objects, you are only going to make $5. Whereas you only have to sell *one* $10 object to make $5. Or $10 on a $20 object. And how about a $100 art deco statuette or a $150 lamp, paperweight, et cetera. What is the point in spending your time and only making peanuts.

Now what Pop brings home to Mom from auctions isn't stuff that he can't sell to dealers, but things that he can't get *enough* for from dealers. And, of course, if Mom finds out that Pop was wrong about how much the object is worth, back it goes into his station wagon to unload to a dealer for whatever he can get for it.

Now there is another hidden value in Mom running a parlor shop while Pop is out running around in his station wagon doubling his money every sixty days. And that is that you are building up a stock that you can both take to antique shows or, as mentioned above, use for a mail-order operation. And both of these options are far commoner ways to make a good living than people not in the business usually realize. Everybody thinks first of olde antique shoppes. But only about a quarter of the money that is made in the antiques business is made through shops. The other three quarters of it is made by selling at shows, selling through ads in the trade press and, of course, by the wheeler-dealers who double their money in sixty days that most of this book is about.

So I think these auxiliary operations are important to know about, especially if Pop has a Mom to run them while he is out on the road doubling his money every sixty days. So for what it's worth, that's my rationale for this chapter and the two following ones, "Selling Through Ads in the Trade Press" and "Selling at Antique Shows."

Selling Through Ads in the Trade Press

This way of selling is a lot easier than it might seem to be. And ads in the trade publications are especially important when you find something really good, which is to say that it is more valuable than the things usually handled by the dealers you usually serve. So it needs wider exposure to get the best price.

Now here is how this works. If the item is Victorian, you advertise it in *The Antiques Trader Weekly.* If it is Early American, you advertise in *The Maine Antique Digest.* And if it is art deco, art nouveau or French or English, you advertise it in *The Antiques and Arts Weekly.* Addresses are listed in the back of this book, and just ask for the advertising department.

You don't, of course, put a price on it, because all the dealers and decorators who subscribe to these publications will understand that you are putting the piece up for telephone bids. And they won't waste their money to call you by fooling around. They will make you their real, highest-possible bid. They will also be honest about paying you, because they would be ruined in a month when the word got around that they weren't playing the game the way it is supposed to be played.

Selling at Antique Shows

The big thing that you regular people out there don't understand about antique shows is that the dealers are not there to sell their stuff to you regular people, but to sell their stuff to each other. In other words, an antique show is a powwow of dealers who have gathered together to trade with each other and do some social visiting and lie swapping.

So there is nothing the matter with a get-rich-quick person like you doing the same thing. After you have accumulated enough unsold oddities, junk and "dogs" to overfill a booth, you take them to an antique show with the sure knowledge that every other dealer in the show will stop by to see what you have that they have the slightest chance of selling "back home"—wherever that may be. If only because they have sold some of the stuff they brought with them and it would be a waste of space not to fully pack their station wagon for the trip back home.

Pricing your objects is handled this way: If you know what the object is worth, you put double that amount on it. That's in case someone in the great general public of regular people has a mad lust for such things. All the other dealers will understand that you will sell it to them for half that price.

And here's the best part. If you have something that you don't know the value of, you don't put a price sticker on it. Then when any dealer asks you for the price, you can admit that you don't know and ask him to make an offer. No embarrassment. No trick. You're just trying to find out what something is worth. And the dealer will understand what you are doing, and that you will be doing it with the other dealers at the show, too.

So after you have gotten a few offers, you go to the booth of the dealer who made the best one and sell him your treasure. Or hold out—if you have any idea of where you could get more from, say, an interior decorator. But at least you know what you have got and some idea of its value.

And, of course, there is another advantage of having all those doubled prices on your stuff. If one of the regular people looks at one of your prices and wags his head sadly, you can jump in the breach and say, "You know, I need space in my station wagon, and I could come down a lot on that." Et cetera, et cetera and blah, blah, blah. (Oh, so you are deceitful, too, are you?)

Where to Buy Good Stuff Cheap

The new wholesale marketplace for the whole country where everybody goes three times a year

It used to be a lot harder than it is now. Because about ten years ago the antiques business finally got its act together and developed a single wholesale marketplace for the whole country. What happened was that a man named Gordon Reid owned a nice-sized farm in the middle of a great flat valley that spreads easterly from the tiny village of Brimfield, Massachusetts. And not having much to do one summer, he decided to open a flea market in one of the nice flat fields next to his house.

Naturally everybody said he was crazy because Brimfield is in the middle of nowhere and has only one lonely country road that passes through the valley. But Gordon Reid knew a lot of antique dealers, and knew how to talk people into doing things he wanted them to do. So about fifty dealers showed up one weekend that summer. No customers, of course, because nobody had ever heard of Brimfield in those days, and precious few people ever drove along that country road through the valley so that they could see the sign FLEA MARKET that he had hung out. But something else happened of far more importance. Not being bothered by any customers from the civilian population, those fifty dealers went crazy selling everything they had to each other.

The reason for this is that one dealer had fifty baskets that were all the same size, so all the other dealers bought a couple of them from him at rock-bottom prices to fill out their stock. A toy dealer showed up, so every dealer who needed some toys to fill out their stock bought a couple of toys from him: et cetera, et cetera. And so while nobody made any money, when the market was over, everybody went home happy as pigs in mud.

Well, since antique dealers are constantly traveling around and none of them ever stops talking, the news spread like wildfire that Brimfield was the place to get rid of what you didn't need and to find what you did need at "dealers' prices." (Incidentally, even when not at Brimfield, all dealers sell to each other at heavy discounts simply because they want you to do the same for them. It is as if the whole business was one big private club.)

The rest, as they say, is history. Today there are ten different flea markets on the farms that border Route 20, the road that runs through Brimfield's great flat valley. And during the second weeks of May, July and September over two thousand antique dealers—no junk or trash dealers allowed—congregate from all over the country to buy and sell from each other at wholesale prices. And at least another two thousand stop by to shop for the things they need to supply their customers.

So if anybody ever tells you we are running out of antiques, just tell them to take a walk through Brimfield—where they can see $10 million worth of them for sale three times a year. (It's simple mathematics. The average dealer brings about $5,000 worth of stock. And 2,000 times $5,000 is $10 million every time.)

So this is what it is like and what you should do when you go there. Bring money. At least $2,000. But there is also a local bank that will give you cash on your Visa card. If you tell them why you need it, *your* bank will raise your cash limit on your card to $2,500. Many successful operators—hundreds of them—arrive in Brimfield with no less than $10,000 cash in their pockets. (Like I said—no junk.)

Naturally you will have to come in a station wagon or van to put your loot into—also to sleep in. That's because for every Brimfield week all motel rooms within a fifty-mile radius have already been reserved by people who are diffident about sleeping in vans. But there *is* a campground a few miles west of Brimfield on Route 20, which always has a space near their shower building (nice and clean) where you can pitch a tent.

There are some places open at the beginning of the week, but the real action begins on Wednesday morning when a line up of 350 trucks packed to overflowing pours into the May's field (next to Gordon Reid's field) at ten-thirty in the morning. And what a scramble that is with everybody running around waving money at each other to get what they think is the cream of the crop. The other big fields open on Thursday and Friday, and you have to see it to believe it. There is no chance of your even just walking past all those two thousand spaces, as they are called, much less considering them all. That's why you will see things like four young men come out of a truck from Texas with walkie-talkies in their hands. Each one covers a section of the field and they all confer on their wavelength about what each of them has found.

So all you have to do is look for our recommended fastest-selling objects—or your selections of what interests you most from the list—and buy them as you find them with a pretty certain knowledge that you can sell them at a 50 to 100 percent markup to your string of dealers that you are supplying because they don't have the energy to go to Brimfield. Of course, sometimes you will get stuck and other times you will make a killing, but that's the excitement of the antiques business.

The Truth About Refinishing

Or, where were you when I really needed you, Homer Formsby

Well, I have to laugh every time I see Homer Formsby do his "instant refinishing" trick on one of his television commercials. I think it is because he makes refinishing look so easy. And so clean—no Gunk before the Glow. But I suppose I'm just jealous, because I used to be a homey little old furniture doctor myself. And *I* wasn't able to start a multimillion dollar business in refinishing supplies on the side, and still have time left over to make my own $3,000-a-minute commercials—he has it all over me!

But getting back to the point of this book, you're not going to make any money buying and selling furniture that you have to refinish between the buying and the selling. EXCEPT when it *really* is easy.

And that happy circumstance occurs when the piece you have was finished only with shellac, which was the only finish anybody had up until about 1850. After which much tougher lacquers and varnishes were used and are still being invented.

But shellac has the marvelous quality—for us—of

immediately dissolving when touched by alcohol. This is because shellac is made by dissolving the resin from some tree in India in alcohol in the first place. So it is a terrible finish to spill martinis on, but a wonderfully easy one to remove. And even when you do remove it, enough of it will remain in the fiber of the wood to "seal" the surface of the wood so that you do not need to apply any new finish. All you have to do is wax the surface for a soft luster—or apply an oil polish for a brighter look, as you prefer.

So how do you tell if a piece has shellac on it or not? Well, after a while you will be able to tell by looking at it. But one test is that it will crack easily if you press the edge of a coin on it. Shellac is brittle. Or you can keep a small can of denatured alcohol in your station wagon and apply a few drops with your finger. If it is shellac, it will dissolve in three seconds or less. Varnishes are more elastic and dent but do not crack.

So given that you have bought and brought home an old table that has dirty, grimy, cracked and white-spotted shellac on it, what do you do? You take it out into your backyard and put it on an old picnic table that you use for such gunky work—which Homer Formsby never tells you about in his commercials.

Then you go down to your local paint and hardware store and buy a gallon of denatured alcohol—enough for three or four tables, but it comes cheaper by the gallon. Also a package of 000 (fine but not too fine) steel wool. This you unroll a pad at a time and, making smaller pads out of it, dip into the alcohol to gently scrub the shellac finish off the wood—squeezing the shellac out of the pad as it gets filled with it. Men usually use their bare rough hands and women wear rubber gloves. Unless you are a tough woman with rough hands.

One trick that will conserve your alcohol is to put a two-quart bowl underneath each leg as you work on it to catch the alcohol as it runs down the leg you are scrubbing.

For the finishing touches, use a cloth pad dipped in the alcohol and wrung out for a final wipe-down of the whole piece. Then, if the original finish is in good shape, leave it as it prettily is or you can wax and polish it. To give the piece a supersoft look, gently wipe the piece down with a pad of extra-fine dry steel wool during the waxing and polishing stage. *Chacun a son goût*, you old fool. I mean me, not you.

Regional Sellers

And the trucks are out there rolling every day of the week

There are many people—usually families—that make a living in the antiques business by simply moving antiques from one part of the country to another. With the big boys even moving them from one continent to another.

This is made possible by the fact that we are a regional country, with each region having a different cultural history.

One of the most obvious examples of this regionalism is that an old ox-yoke that sells for $25 in Nova Scotia because it's a pretty common object will be bought in Texas for $250 to $350 because, as I pointed out earlier, Texans like to hang one over their mantelpiece and claim that it is the very same ox-yoke that their great granddaddy used when he came to settle the state. The same thing goes for old wooden farm-wagon wheels from anywhere in the back country of the Eastern states. Buggy seats are another hot item in Texas, as is anything made out of oak, which Texans consider to be Early American. And because of this, the trucks are rolling back and forth from Providence, Rhode Island, and Wheeling,

West Virginia, out to Texas every day, Saturdays and Sundays included.

Another fundamental regional preference is that of American Empire furniture of the Victorian Era, which is much in demand in Georgia. This is the bulky pine-covered furniture with good figured mahogany veneer and simple round curves, which is just old furniture everywhere except in Georgia, where it is the style the South refurnished its houses with after General Sherman burned all the stuff they had before that. So the trucks roll back and forth from New England to Atlanta with that.

Victorian oak furniture also sells for three times as much in the Midwest as it does in the states along the Eastern coast. For the obvious reason that the Midwest was settled after the Eastern states so that oak is what Great Granddaddy had when he started his tool factory or hog-butchering plant.

Primitive furniture sells best in Virginia and the Northeastern states.

And what do you think goes at a premium in southern California? Strangely enough it is ornate, rococo French chests, bureaus, clocks, chandeliers—the stuff you see in movies about decadence in the French court of Louis XVI with Marie Antoinette telling the peasants to eat cake (hardtack) and all that.

Oak furniture, I should also note, sells very high in Manhattan. Just in the center of New York City, not even in the suburbs of the city, and certainly nowhere else in the East.

Also, folk art sells three times higher in New York City than anywhere else. Three times is the average markup on it between the antique flea market at

Brimfield, Massachusetts, and The Fall Antiques Show on Pier 90 in New York City every October. (See the section on folk art in Part II.)

All the unwanted clocks, boxes and bric-a-brac that have come to this country from central Europe and Germany end up in a group of dingy starvation shops in Delray Beach, Florida. It's not a very profitable trade for you to get into, but I just thought you might want to know so you don't waste any time going there.

Old cameras go best—by far the best—in the big cities of the Northeast—Boston, Providence, New York, Philadelphia, Pittsburgh.

Nothing sells in Buffalo, New York. Of course, nothing happens there either. But it is a good source for oak office furniture—as is Providence, Rhode Island.

And so it goes. I sure don't know everything about this, but I think you can get the general idea from these meanderings.

How to Sell Antiques to Dealers

Back in the Middle Ages when I was a young man, I used to be an assistant sales manager for Remington Rand in their typewriter division. And we had three rules on the craft of selling that we had to teach all our salesmen who were going out from office to office trying to sell Remington Rand typewriters to the bosses who ran them.

The first one was to warm up the prospect by always asking him a series of questions that he had to say "yes" to, to get him in an affirmative frame of mind. Such as: Do you love your children? Is life hard? Would you like to run away to Bermuda with one of the girls in the typing pool? Ordinary things like that, which any boss would have to say yes to. To get the prospect in an affirmative frame of mind. We were a progressive company that believed in psychology.

The second rule, which I discussed earlier, was that they should never ask a boss to buy only one model of typewriter, because that gave him the option to say no. So what we had our salesmen do was to show the boss two different typewriters, pointing out the different features of both of them. Then while he was considering the differences between the two typewriters, they would ask the boss which one he thought was the best one for his particular needs.

When the sucker chose one over the other, our salesman would write his name down on his order pad and push it over to the boss for his signature. Oh, some people are so deceitful. And we had some star salesmen out there for whom the trick never failed.

And the third trick was that if the boss hesitated about signing the order blank, our salesman would say, "And, oh yes, this is the one that comes with our *free* booklet on how to get along with your secretary." Or whatever, but something unexpected for *free.* Like the booklet that cost us 25 cents.

So all you have to do is transfer this scene to the tailgate of your station wagon, substituting antiques for typewriters. It's fun. It's the selling game. And you aren't actually cheating anybody, so what can you lose?

Buying Antiques for a Retirement Nest Egg

Even if I am unable to learn anything about antique jewelry

About ten years ago my wife and I bought a cobbler's bench for $125. We use it as a cocktail table in front of a couch. Today it is worth at least $350 at any good auction. And we needed a table in front of that couch anyway.

And we have also gradually replaced all of our old furniture with antiques, too. All of which appreciates in value at about the same rate that that cobbler's bench does. I am talking about chairs, end tables, drop-leaf tables, couches, beds, bookcases, the whole kit-and-kaboodle.

So when it comes time for us to retire to Florida or Mexico as old people should to keep warm, we will call in our local auctioneer of "the good stuff" to take it all away in his truck to put up at one of his auctions. And after the auction, he will give us a check for many, many times what we would get for just a houseful of used furniture.

In fact, my wife has gone even further, because we have a garage and she has this almost filled up with what she calls her "collection," which will sell for even more than our furniture.

Of course, there are things you can buy for a retirement nest egg that don't take up as much space as my wife's eclectic collection. Antique jewelry is the first thing that comes to my mind, but then I don't know anything about it and I don't seem to be able to learn anything either. But I do know that you should pick something that you can learn something about. Because becoming an expert through doing some buying and selling as well as building up your collection . . . well, that's obvious, isn't it.

Offhand, some of the other things you could specialize in are painted lead soldiers, hand-painted miniatures, lithographed tin toys, brass statuettes, clocks, decoys, dolls, folk art, watercolor portraits.

The way to decide what you want to deal in and collect is to start going to antique shows and find out what kinds of objects you "lust" for. Then there are magazines and price guides extant for almost anything you can think of, and you can find out what they are and how to get them by simply asking the dealers who display them at their booths.

But there is something I do know about any specialty that you choose. And that is that as you learn about your specialty you should always move toward dealing in the top-of-the-line objects in it. Because in any line the rarest and therefore the most expensive pieces will appreciate in relative value faster than the poor, average and good classifications. I suppose you could call it the rarity factor, which merely "good" pieces can never have. The scramble among rich collectors is always to own "the finest" so that they can brag to their friends and show off to their poor relatives.

For myself, I collect folk art because it is a very, very snobbish specialty that is patronized by very rich people such as stockbrokers and orthodontists, who are easy to fool. For more about this, see my discourse on folk art in Part II of this book.

Part II

THE 45 FASTEST-SELLING ANTIQUES THAT YOU CAN BUY AND SELL FOR A QUICK PROFIT

Advertising and ephemera

From Coca-Cola trays to valentines

The fastest-selling antiques range from Coca-Cola trays to old circus and early movie posters.

As to the trays, by now there are far more reproductions of old ones put out by the Coca-Cola company itself than there are old ones around. So signs of wear and a little bit of rust are important, and the rust shouldn't be removed. At least, not by you.

As to the paper and cardboard posters, these are going so cheaply that there isn't much chance for you to make any significant profit on them. Unless, of course, you just buy the most interesting of them and frame them. For which purpose you will also have to get into buying old frames with glass still in them.

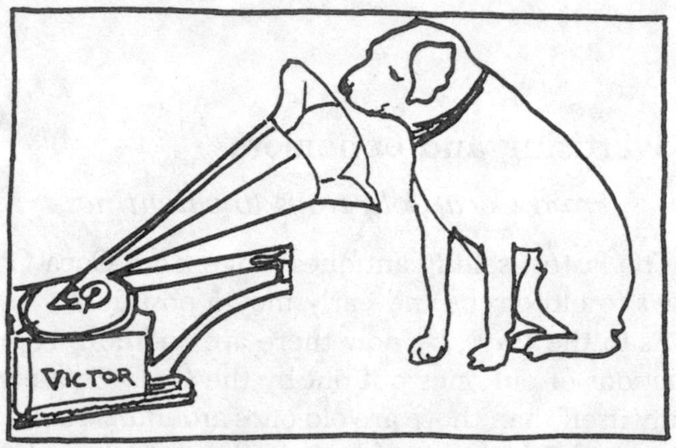

This means that you have to be something of a handyman (oops, handyperson!), but a $3 or $4 piece of paper in a $2 frame has got to be worth $25. So the attention you paid to something interesting has created a new value.

Naturally the same thing applies to framing valentines, sheet music, old magazine covers and old advertising posters, all of which are generally called *ephemera,* and framing them on long winter nights is a nice little specialty to have.

Andirons and fire tools

You ought to buy all pairs of andirons and sets of fire tools that have any brass on them. Not because you can sell them to antique dealers, because you can't. They don't move in antique stores, because the kind of people who go to antique stores already have their andirons, etc., already standing by the old fireplaces of their rickety old antique houses.

But people who have just bought a new $150,000 house will have fireplaces with nothing in them, and so with a little effort you can find a nice curving road through a development where all the families in those nice expensive houses need andirons and fireplace tools. And these are houses in which they are sitting and waiting for you to knock on their door every Sunday afternoon. So mark your andirons up to twice what you paid for them. Otherwise people like these will think your andirons aren't expensive enough to go into their nice, new expensive houses.

Simple iron andirons that were handmade by blacksmiths are authentic Early American antiques and are a lot rarer than the decorated brass ones. But only real antiquarians are interested in them. As a result, the demand for them is light and they are not worth tying up your money in.

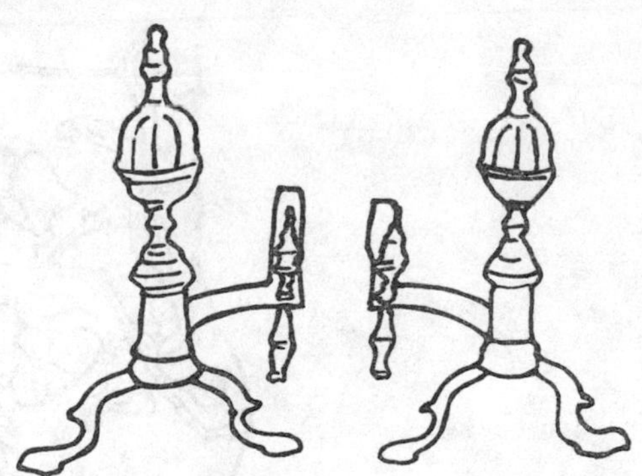

Art pottery and chinaware

You can often find these items at flea markets and garage sales, and you can usually mark them up ten times more than what you paid, but the problem is in telling you what they look like and how to evaluate them because they are so darned varied and new to the marketplace. Art pottery is basically vases, bowls, pitchers, platters and even some sets of chinaware that were made in small potteries between 1900 and 1945 or 1950. They were designed for the gift store market, and as time went by, some of the potteries were so successful that they grew into small factories, keeping their original designs but cutting down on the handwork and eliminating the signatures that the original potters used. Some of the better-known producers of this stuff were S.E.G., Peters & Reed and Rookwood. And prices for pieces by such makers range in the $50 to $150 class—but some go up into

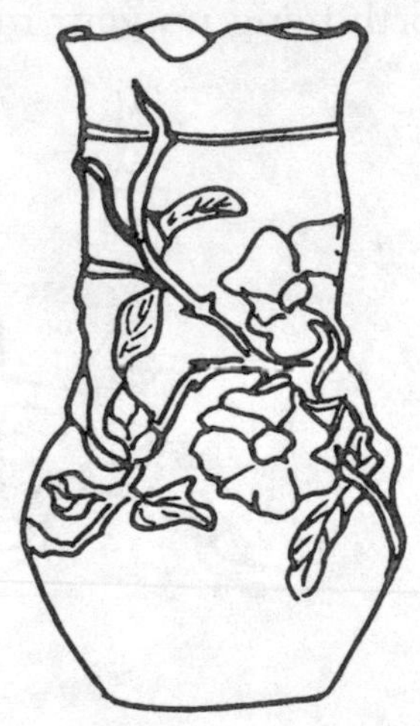

the thousands. However, the whole field is still wide open as to what is and isn't art pottery and how much it is worth—making it another excellent class of object to deal in for frequently high markups if you have an eye for whatever "art" is.

Some people make a big mystery out of that, and say that you either know what art is or you don't and never the twain shall meet. You have artistic taste or you don't. But that's not so. Or why would they have art schools?

What makes a good piece of art pottery can be judged by the following principles:

1. A harmonious combination of colors. Colors that don't conflict and jar the nerves of your retina. A combination that in fact delights the nerves of your retina. This can be studied with a color wheel of the spectrum. But all that does is prove what the nerves of the retina sense immediately.

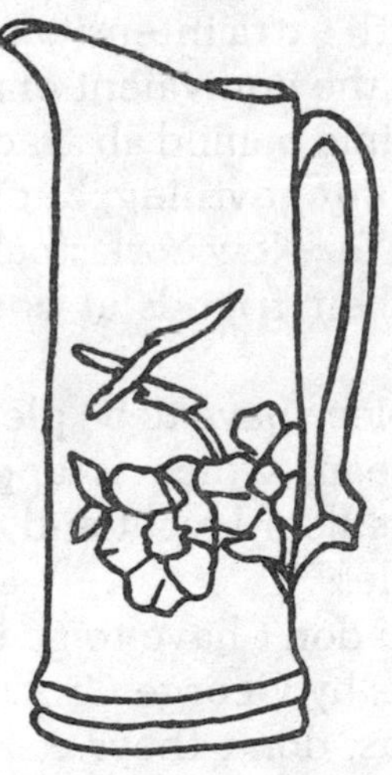

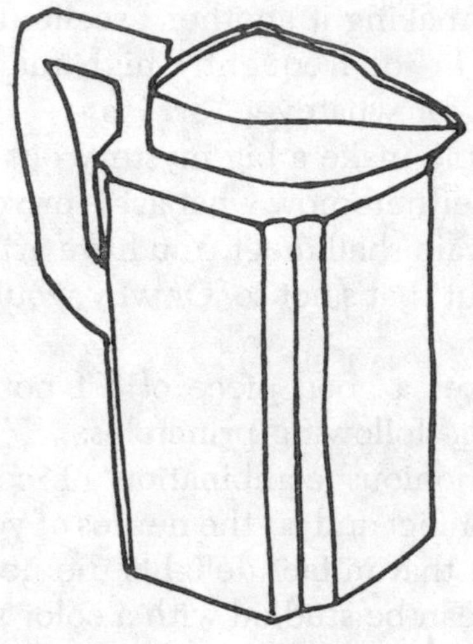

2. The amount of mass of the different colors should balance each other with extra intensity of any color being considered to be the equivalent of more mass. That is the whole principle behind abstractions —those "pictures" that aren't *of* anything, but some artists get rich painting them for New York stockbrokers who want to impress their friends at cocktail parties.

3. The proportions of the piece have to be pleasing in terms of The Golden Mean, which is approximately five by seven, as in the floor layout and other parts of the old Greek temples.

See how easy it is. Now you don't have to go to art school. People who buy books by George Grotz sure get a lot of free extra benefits, don't they?

Banks, cast-iron

Caveat emptor, and let your conscience be your guide

The best kind are the ones where you push a coin in a slot and that makes one of the figures move—like Punch hitting Judy with a bat. Or a spring that you release makes a hunter shoot a penny into a hole in a tree. Originally these were made for fun by foundries that spent most of their time casting iron stoves. And these are pretty rare so they have well-established values which are listed in any good price guide, such as "Warman's." All are in the hundreds, some over $1,000.

But then in the 1920s an encyclopedia company decided to mass-reproduce twelve banks—to use as premiums to promote the sale of their encyclopedias. And they did a wonderfully good job, even with the colors of paint that were hand applied.

Of course these reproductions originally looked newer than the original ones—but that was sixty years ago. And distressing them by pulling rusty old tire chains over them has helped quite a few of them to look a lot older in a hurry. There are also slight differences where the new molds joined, but these projections can also be ground down and smoothed off with emery paper.

So add to this that there are an awful lot of liars in the world and the result is total confusion.

But in that confusion lurks opportunity. Since authenticity has become such a matter of opinion, all you have to do is adapt a policy of buying the reproductions in the $60 to $75 range and only selling originals in the $350 to $900 range. It works out nicely, doesn't it.

There are also many kinds of "nonaction" cast-iron banks—all kinds of animals, mammy dolls and especially small bank buildings. These retail in the $30 to $80 range, and if you buy them at an auction or antiques flea market, you can put 15 to 20 percent markup for your quick resale to your antique shop dealers. That's nothing spectacular, but banks are good, fast-moving, bread-and-butter items that don't take up much room in your station wagon.

Barbershop things

Not to mention old dentists' chairs, too

Barber poles are wonderful. Hard to fake, too, because you need a lathe to make the good old wooden ones. But men who don't like any other kind of antiques at all like barber poles. And everybody who likes folk art likes barber poles. And shaving mugs with pictures of occupations on them, and mustache cups that keep the coffee out of your mustache—and even barber chairs for downstairs in the playroom.

So this is the real manly stuff—as opposed to sissy English furniture like Adams and Hepplewhite. But it is very fast-selling because there is so little in the antiques marketplace that would appeal to Norman Mailer and Rip Torn and all those other tough guys.

So the obvious place to sell these is at your local V.F.W. bar or the Elks, K. of C., Moose, Volunteer Fire Department and all such places that men gather. And dentists are particularly hot for old dentist chairs for their playrooms in the cellar.

Also if you ever notice a barber shop quartette

mentioned in your local newspapers, these good fellows are almost always collectors of related objects and pay you a good price for them.

Baskets—splint and wicker

What to look for and how to repair them in two half hours

One thing about buying baskets is that they are good for carrying around the other things you buy. And another is that if you are any good at all at fixing things, you can make terrific money by buying all the dirty, old, broken ones that you see from dumb dealers for a dollar or two.

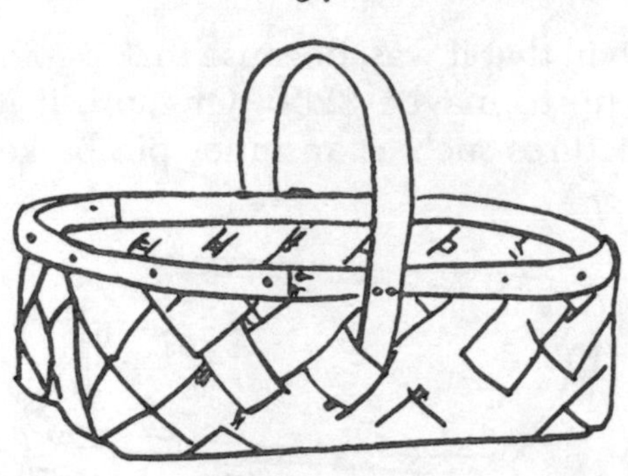

Obviously the first thing you do with a basket—wicker or splints of oak, hickory or ash—is to scrub it with soapy water. But preserve any old paint that you find on one, because that makes it more valuable—maybe around 100 percent!

Then the trick is that while it is still wet, you pin the broken pieces back in place with push pins so that the pieces will dry in position. Then in a few days when the basket is really dry, you pull out the pins and glue the broken pieces in place with Elmer's Glue-All or Elmer's Carpenter's Glue, sticking the push pins back in to hold the pieces in place while the glue dries. And such repairs will never be noticed or even seen without a magnifying glass.

So in a couple of half hours you can turn a $2 basket back into a $35 to $60 one.

What we are talking about are common baskets used for laundry, storage, picnics, carrying vegetables and eggs, gathering berries. But if you run across a shallow, rectangular one that is tightly woven with fine reeds, you have a find, because there is a good chance that it was made by the Shakers. And once you have bought it, you will start becoming increasingly certain that it was, because that is going to push its value up to maybe $250. Or more if it has any special features such as an inner pin basket or handles.

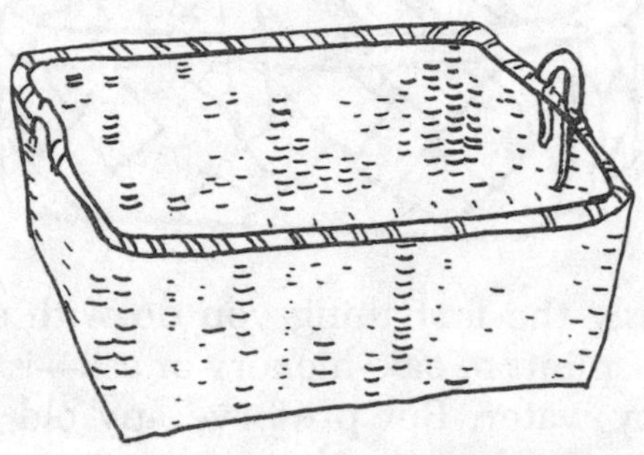

The way you tell the age of a basket is that the older wicker ones were made from the long trailing branches of willow trees, the later ones from imported reed that is perfectly regular in dimension.

There is also a way to tell a really old splint basket from one made after around 1830. The earlier ones are made of splint cut by hand from ax-split pieces of ash or hickory. As a result, the splints are of irregular thickness and width. But because baskets have such a common tendency to wear out, these really old ones are rare and belong in your local historical society.

After 1830, of course, the splints were cut in a factory, which is why they are regular. The baskets were still made by hand though, because other things happened before anybody got around to inventing a basket-making machine.

Bedside tables

Standard items, but sure sellers

Bedside tables—four legs and one drawer—are always good to bid on at an auction. If there are several

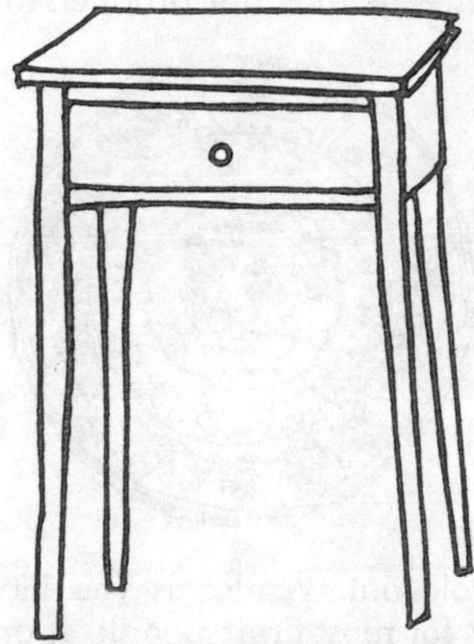

being put up for sale, you just bid on the last one—in the hope that any dealer lust has by then been satisfied. These are also easy to reglue and even to refinish if you can get a crummy one really cheaply. But it is a more practical use of your time to just rub them down with mineral spirits and 000 steel wool and then wipe them with Old English brown-oil polish.

Anyway, they are good movers and not too big to be hauling in and out of your station wagon to show to dealers.

Blue plates

The secret of buying china without knowing anything about it

I once knew a lady who was a very good potter. And every time she took her produce to a crafts fair,

she always sold out. While, as you have doubtless noticed, sales for most craftspeople at crafts fairs are painfully desultory because all craftsmen and craftsladies are on ego trips.

So I asked her one day why she thought her pottery sold so much better than all the potter's pottery. And she said to me, "Haven't you noticed, George, it's all blue."

And I conceded that, yes, I had noticed that it was all covered with a beautiful cobalt blue glaze. But what, I asked did that have to do with anything?

"Anything blue always sells," says she.

"Why?" says I.

"I don't know," says she. "I think people just like blue."

And the same thing goes for antique chinaware—flow blue, transfer blue, Dutch blue, anything blue.

So given that it is reasonably priced according to your handy "Warman's" price guide—i.e., about half the Warman listing—blue is what you look for and blue is what you buy for a sure and quick turnover.

Why? Because people like blue, of course.

In your favorite price guide ("Warman's" is by far the best), you will find blue plates under "Flow Blue," which is obvious, and transfer plates. Transfer plates are the familiar blue ones with little pictures of life in a Chinese garden. The pictures were printed on thin sheets of paper with lots of ink that was then pressed onto the wet clay paint before it was fired and then glazed with a thin coating of glass. The transfers were applied in sections, and you can always detect slight mismatches where the lines are supposed to join.

Flow blue is gorgeous, because the blue dye painted on the moist clay plate really flows in the firing process to give a luscious look. And, of course, no two plates are exactly alike, giving you the option of claiming that the one you are selling is far more beautiful than any other you have seen and that you are therefore forced by your conscience to get a little bit more for it to help pay for the operation your grandmother in traction needs so that she can walk again.

Brass beds

Oh, how those interior decorators lust for them!

I know brass beds won't fit inside your station wagon, but you can tie them to a rack on top, can't you? And when you find one, don't waste any time trying to sell it to antiques dealers. Instead, telephone a list of interior decorators, taken from the Yellow Pages of the nearest city of any size, and tell them what you have. Interior decorators love brass beds, and you should hold them up for a really good price because the decorators will sell them for a lot more to their rich clients.

Candlestands

Oh, how I love those candlestands. And not just because they don't wobble when you put them on an uneven floor. Which is why they have only three legs, of course. What I like about them is that every one is different, having been made by country cabinetmakers, so that we have here another item whose value is in the eye of the beholder and a matter of opinion.

There are fakes galore, of course, because they are an easy piece for any cabinetmaker to produce. For this reason an old crackled or cracked finish is the best way to tell a genuine piece. Another way to tell a fake is by the wood not having shrunken across the grain over the last 150 to 200 years. For instance, a round tabletop should measure a half inch less across

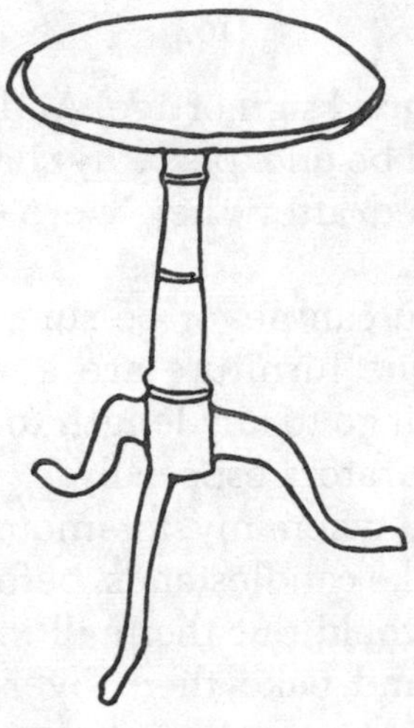

the grain than along the grain. The central post will also no longer be perfectly round, but you will need a caliper to detect this as the shrinkage will be only about a sixteenth of an inch. A metal brace on the bottom of the post to hold the legs in against the post

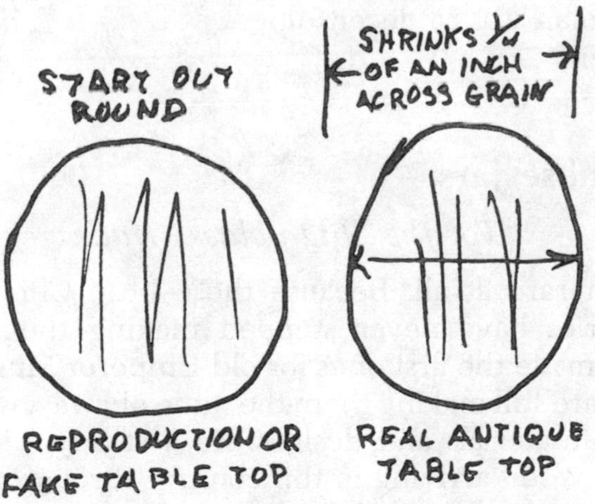

is also another good sign of age. And the turnings on the posts should be unexpectedly sharp because they were not sanded after they were taken from the lathe.

However, you can never be sure about anything. Fakers of antique furniture are a gleeful bunch of fanatics that will go to any length to fool rich people and museum curators especially.

For instance, when my infamous Uncle George used to make fake candlestands, before he assembled the pieces he would put them all in the oven of his kitchen stove and bake them overnight at around three hundred degrees. Sometimes he'd bake them for two nights if the oven hadn't stayed hot enough, until the tops had shrunk at least three sixteenths of an inch across the grain.

This baking also dried out the surface fibers of the wood so that when he shellacked it he had an instant 200-year-old patina showing through the finish. Oh, that man was so deceitful!

Chinese jars

For the "high-class" trade

Not rare at all. Because those little Chinese jar factories have never stopped making them since they made the first ones for old Emperor Ming. And they are still making them the same old way, with the same materials and designs. So a steady trickle of them is still arriving in this country through men in our merchant marine fleet.

These fellows buy them for a few dollars and sell them as soon as they get back to a U.S. port. They will pay, say, $25 for something that ends up retailing for $459 to $600. The truly old ones—which take an expert to identify—naturally go for higher amounts, but that is a separate trade carried by international art dealers.

These jars sell great to interior decorators and the "high-class" antique dealers in the bigger cities and especially in Washington, D.C. And since they are all different, owing to the hand painting of the designs, there is always some doubt about how much each one is worth. So when offering one for sale, always first ask three times what you paid for it. You may have gotten a bargain, and the dealer may know more about it than you do. Of course, if he grabs it at your three-times markup, you'll never stop wondering how much more you should have asked.

Copper and brass buckets

Which you can resell at a really good markup to the same place you sold the andirons and fire tools

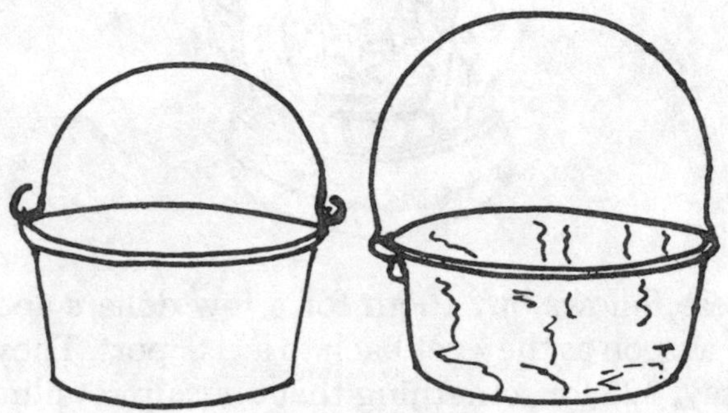

These sell like andirons and fire tools. They are very slow movers in antique shops, but hot stuff on Sunday afternoons in the suburbs. Because the same people who need andirons in their new fireplaces also need copper and brass buckets to sit next to them to hold coal or kindling wood. So instead of my going over the whole thing again, why don't you just turn to the section on andirons and fire tools.

Decorated boxes

With sailboats and eagles and American flags and all that good stuff

Buy all the old wooden and tin boxes you ever see at flea markets. Just stack them up in a dark corner until you have about thirty of them. Then go to art school and learn to paint eagles and sailboats and American flags and whales spouting—all that good stuff.

After the paint is dry, put them on a table and beat them with some bicycle lock chains to get dents and chips in the paint. Then rub them with some walnut or burnt umber stain and put them out in the sun to dry. In fact, leave them out for about a year.

Finally take them—only showing one at a time, mind you—to some big-city antique shops and sell them for $350 a piece.

Of course, if you are zero on artistic talent, you will have to find some nice little old lady at your local church crafts fair to do the painting for you. But you do the chain distressing and walnut glazing yourself.

You think I jest. No, I don't. It's a jungle out there, Petunia, and there just aren't enough decorated antique boxes to go around to make all the people who lust for them happy. So you make them happy. Could God blame you for that? And God wants all his children to have money, too. Or why would He have made so many movie stars and other rich people?

Desks, ladies'

Where everything goes, and how to buy them cheaply at auctions

One time a nice lady asked a famous auctioneer how he decided on what things he bought to furnish

his own house. He thought about that for a while, and then he asked her, "Lady, did you ever lust for an object?"

Well, even the nicest ladies lust for small ladies' desks—in which they can get all their papers, bills, letters, recipes, school report cards and everything else together in one place.

Of course, these are rarely found at flea markets;

you have to go back one step in the line of supply to the auctions. And then whenever one comes up, the nice ladies bid against each other, driving them up to far higher prices than any dealer would pay. And the winning lady takes her desk home and keeps it—out of the antiques business forever. Even after she dies, because one of her daughters grabs it then.

So you can never make any profit trying to outbid lustful ladies. But you are reasonably safe in bidding against another dealer when none of those ladies has shown up.

Another point worth making is that the smaller the desk, the better. Not just because it will take up less space in your station wagon, but because the smaller they are, the more popular they are. And children's desks are best of all.

But the most important thing of all for you to understand is that in dealing with desks, old age is not the factor that it is with other classifications of objects. Sure antique ones are swell. But the demand for desks is so great that anything goes with them: good handmade reproductions, good Grand Rapids reproductions, terrible North Carolina reproductions that are way off the original style, anything!

Dolls

Every spring, midsummer and early fall some nice family—I think their name is Gurley—puts on a really good antiques flea market at the fairgrounds up in Cumberland, Maine. Well over a hundred dealers arrive at dawn with station wagons packed full of good stuff that they use to set up shops in the open livestock sheds. So if it doesn't rain, it is a great party as lots of the dealers know each other and the pickers

come to buy stuff to take back to sell to their antique dealers all over the Northeastern states.

Well, I don't know hardly anything about dolls, but last summer up in Cumberland I saw a black mammy doll made on an old bottle for $40 and a topsy-turvy doll for only $35. And they just looked like too much fun to pass up. So when I got home I looked them up in my Knopf collectors' guide to dolls, and there they were on pages 30 and 31 in full color, and priced in the back of the book at $150 to $225. And since I could sell them to any dealer for at least half the price guide price, I had a $40 profit in each of them. Of course my wife took them away from me and put them in her early retirement collection, but what can I tell you. I just can't say no to a beautiful woman.

So if I had sold them on the way home instead of showing them to my wife, I could have doubled my money the next day. A lucky buy? Maybe a little, but dolls are such fast sellers they are always worth taking a chance on.

Duck decoys

The trick is to be sure you call them folk art—$$$$!

The world of decoys in three parts divided is:

At the top level we have the works of art. These are carved out of wood to be sculptured interpretations of the bird they represent, and then are as finely painted as the famous Audubon prints of the birds of North America. So the artistic ability of the maker is more important than the age of the piece at this top level. Some of the best date from as late as 1930. And even the work of some living bird-makers is right up there in the $1,500 class. So everybody who collects

THE CRUDER THE BETTER

these things knows the names of the famous makers and they buy them and sell them at secret auctions for members of the club only.

It would take you twenty years to learn enough about these birds to be able to trade in them. This is a very narrow corner in the experience of life. Hardly any of the birds on this top level were actually ever used. They are thought of as artistic interpretations. And some people are just crazy about birds—such as bird-watchers.

The middle level is not only a lot more interesting, but also the one where some good money can be made. This is because these are the birds that were made with love by somebody's Uncle George to actually use to fool flying ducks into landing near them in some swamp while he waited in the bullrushes to shoot them for a delicious roast duck dinner. And all that reality makes these decoys *folk art.* And you know about folk art: it's worth whatever you can get anybody to pay you for it. Aloo-alay, oh, golden day.

So the thing to do with these is to pay $20 to $30 for them and try to get a 50 percent markup from dealers by emphasizing that they are folk art. And settling for 15 percent if you have to. But much more can be made if you take them to the dealers who specialize in folk art who will give you double what you paid for them and then sell them for triple of that. What do I mean *triple?* How about $350 or $450 each?

The best folk art dealers are in Manhattan, because that is where the money is and where Argentinian millionaires go for lunch. Mostly on the Upper East Side along Second Avenue. You can look them up in the Yellow Pages when you get there. Go on a Saturday to avoid the traffic.

On the lowest level you have the factory-made decoys, some terrible canvas things, but these go for such standard prices—low—so low that there is no money to be made in them.

False graining—chests

a. *Early American blanket chests*
b. *Victorian bedroom chests*

One day at a summer auction down in Maine (that's "down" from Boston—all directions from Boston are down) we watched a couple of city slickers and their wives (or maybe mistresses) bid like crazy against each other for an old blanket chest that was falling apart and missing one leg to boot.

But it had a lot of squiggly marks in the old red paint that covered it. So when the auctioneer finally sold the piece, an old fellow who was sitting in front

of me turned to his friend and said, with a touch of wonder in his voice, "I hear they buy the paint."

And so they do.

Because this kind of false graining is not only folk art, but also a fragment of American history, a remnant of the time when this was an agricultural country with 85 percent of its people living on farms. And they made their own paint from skimmed milk and blood drained from hogs when they were hung up by their feet and had their throats cut in the late fall. Which is the way it is still done by people in the back country who still raise a pig or two every year, though few city folks are ever invited to a pig sticking or pig killing, as it is variously called. The hog has to be cut up afterward, of course. It usually takes three men and a quart of whiskey to get it done on a Saturday afternoon.

So you could make a pale paint by using mostly milk or a dark one by using mostly blood. The usual technique was to first apply a solid coat of pale paint. Then when it had dried, you swirled some of the dark around on top of it in an effort to suggest the swirl-grained Honduras mahogany that was the preferred wood of the rich city people in the 1700s.

You'd never guess that that is what they were trying to do, but I once read about it in a book by some antiquarian who has made quite a study of the subject. Rags, feathers, moss, even hands were used to swirl the paint and it often came out stunningly beautiful.

As to making money on this stuff, it is great to buy in the back-country auctions where people aren't all that impressed with it, and take it to some city to sell it. At a large markup.

On the other hand, the false graining on the Victorian bedroom sets was done in the factory with tooth-edged cards, and it has none of the charm and innocence of the early hand-done graining. Some hand graining was also done on interior woodwork. But even that is only imitating oak grain, which is pretty dull.

The furniture was made of pine and sold by mail-order houses in the early 1900s, so there is much of it around. Most of it is still being sanded down with a big belt sander, stained a medium to dark brown, sealed with a coat of shellac and sold as Early American pine. The way to tell these fakes at a glance is that they have paneled sides. The real early pine furniture had solid board sides. These fakes also have obviously machine-cut dovetailing at the ends of the drawers. Lots of little teeth, as opposed to only three or four hand-cut dovetails on the old pieces.

The best of the Victorian false-grained pieces have little hand-painted panels on the front of their drawers, bedsteads, et cetera and because of these there is a small demand for these pieces with the paint still on them by people who feel this sort of decoration should be preserved. But it's a small group, and they can get all they want of this so cheaply that there is little profit to be made in handling this stuff. Unless, of course, you have a big belt sander.

Fancy chairs

The profit lies in spraying them gold

This is a psychology lesson for men.

A fancy chair is a pathetic little spindly chair that looks like it would fall apart if anybody weighing over fifty pounds sat on it. They were made in late Victorian times and sold cheap from wagons that toured the countryside every summer and by mail-order houses. And they sold like crazy.

And they still do, because as pathetic as they are, ladies still love them. Not because they are worth anything as chairs, but because they appeal to the little girl princess that lurks within every grown woman. They remind her of what a fragile feminine thing she really is deep inside.

So having a fancy chair in her bedroom is like having jewelry. And she will love a man who gives her one of these even more than one who brings her flowers.

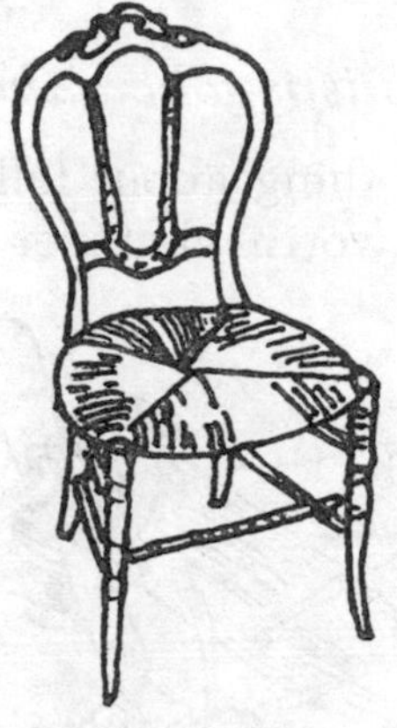

The trick about making money with these things is that no matter how fascinating the remnants of their original decoration is, you heartlessly spray them all over with gold lacquer—as sold in spray cans in your local paint and hardware store. Which makes your $7 purchase worth $45 at retail.

You may also have to reglue some loose rungs and legs, too, but that is easy. And if a rung is missing, it can easily be replaced with a dowel of the exact same size—also from your local hardware store. These come in many diameters, all a yard long, and you just cut them to the needed length.

In case you don't know it, the way to spray-paint a chair is to turn it upside down and spray the inside of the leg structure first. And, of course, you clean the chair first with a detergent and water and let it dry for a few hours before spraying.

Folk art

Real or fake, this is where the big money is

The wonderful thing about folk art, as I've said before, is that it is worth whatever you can get some-

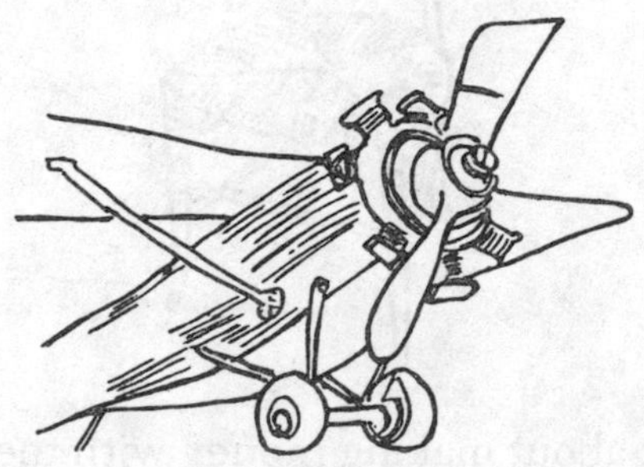

body to pay for it. With the result that there is currently a bull market in it that can only be compared to the stock market in 1928. Like just before 1929, that is! However, while this market lasts, this is where the best money can be made in antiques.

What we are talking about is handmade "country" objects dating anywhere from the early 1700s up to 1935 and, some real promoters claim, even primitive oil paintings still being made.

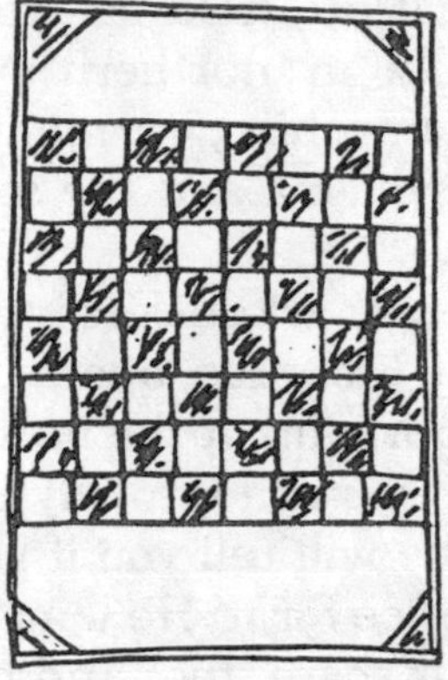

But the basic stock of folk art is: primitive paintings, weathervanes, hand-carved whirligigs, decoys, game boards, wood carvings of farm animals, mammy dolls, baskets, cigar store Indians and other statues and statuettes, trade signs, decorated boxes, gravestones, scrimshaw, false-grained furniture—in other words, works of art done by people who were innocent or unaware of the techniques used by formally trained artists. What my Great-Aunt Louise would have called "pretties" back when she was a folk herself.

And the idea an artist lurks somewhere inside even those of us made of the commonest clay is an appealing one. Especially to effete, Northeastern intellectual snobs, who like to show off to their friends at Park Avenue cocktail parties how *au courant* they are in their artistic taste.

So where can you find such wonderful stuff to deal in that you can mark up from double to ten times what you paid for it? Aye, there's the rub. Unless you already live there, you have to travel to auctions and antique shows that are held far from the madding crowd. Specifically in northern New York state, northern New Hampshire, Vermont and Maine. Or in western Pennsylvania and the southwestern corner of New York.

The king of the folk art dealers is Robert J. Bonner, who with his wife, Florence, operates Bonner's Barn in Malone, New York, up at the northern tip of New York state. And if you run into anything you think is especially good, he will tell you if you are right and give you a good price for it. He'll make his, of course, but you'll get your share, too. And he knows how to promote the stuff he sells. Send him a Polaroid of your object along with a letter about it. The address is: 25 Washington Street, Malone, New York 12953. Look for Bob's two-page ad in *The Maine Antique Digest* if you want to see what class in antiques really is. They are warm people, too, though she's a lot better looking than he is.

Another place you will find folk art is at the great flea markets in Brimfield, held during the second weeks of May, July and September. But since folk art is what sells first, you'll have to get up before dawn to get in on the "flashlight market" that takes place as the dealers from all over the country are unloading. And isn't that a frantic scene with sharpies from New York City running around with flashlights and walkie-talkies to keep in touch with their partners about what each of them has found and how much to pay for it.

Then the best of this stuff is finally sold at retail prices at The Fall Antiques Show at the Pier, on Pier 90 in New York City. Where, according to the fellow I talk to out in the coffee shop in Brimfield Center, fortunes can be made. "They'll buy anything," is the commonest remark. And as one young dealer said, "They will buy anything that was made by human hands. They never get to see anything like that while living in the city."

As to fakes, they are so easy to make and so rampant that the subject just isn't worth talking about anymore. What you see is what you get. And what you think it is, is what it is. So don't upset the apple cart. Everybody is having too good a time making money the way things are right now. In the world of folk art, if you bring up the subject of fakery or suggest that some object might be a fake, people will walk away from you as if you had leprosy. Or the black plague. I've seen it happen. And you can't make any money if people won't talk to you.

For further information about the Fall Antiques Show at Pier 90, write to the organization that sponsors it: Sanford L. Smith and Associates, 152 Second Avenue, New York, NY 10003.

Furniture, country

Or call it primitive pine; it's still a gold mine

Anybody who knows anything about the antiques business will tell you that furniture is where the money is in antiques. But as we said before, for a double-your-money-in-60-days operation, most of it is too big and heavy to get into a station wagon, so us wheeler-dealers have to settle for the smaller pieces

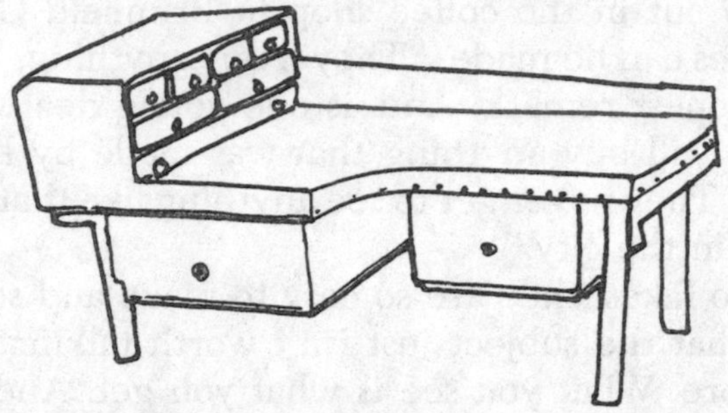

—and a good thing, too, because it is in the small, primitive, country-made furniture that the best profit potential lies.

That is because primitive pieces are one of a kind,

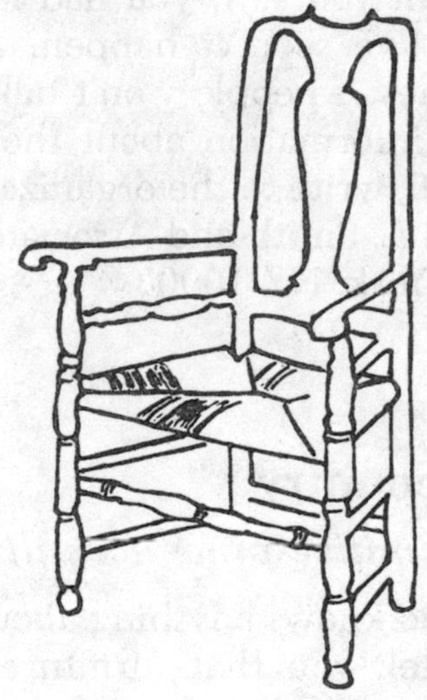

and that makes their value a matter of opinion—within limits, of course.

Let's look at some of the things I am talking about.

Take cobbler's benches, for instance. Almost every one you see come up at an auction is worth buying for a quick-turnover profit. And every third or fourth time you will get lucky and come away with something you can resell for a 50 percent markup. Especially if the seat is split or a leg broken off. These go for so low that your taking the trouble to have them repaired by your local handyman is well worth it. Buying wrecks cheap can be an important part of your operation. And if your local handyman says he doesn't know how to make a new leg match the old ones, buy him a copy of *The Furniture Doctor.*

Another item that is terribly undervalued is the so-called Country Chippendale chair. Many, many of these were made by country carpenters when there was nothing else to do during the snowed-in days of New England winters. And they have great charm to them because they are such sincere attempts to copy the style that was popular in the rich folks' city houses. So they also come in imitation of the Queen Anne and Hepplewhite and Sheraton styles. But the name Country Chippendale caught on because of the nice alliteration. Not that you don't call anything with duck feet Country Queen Anne, et cetera.

So why are they good for trading in? Because like folk art, each is a one-of-a-kind and that puts their value in the eye of the beholder, most of whom don't appreciate them. So the money lies in buying them from those who don't appreciate them and selling them to those who do. Which means moving up the ladder of sophistication from country auctioneers and dealers to big-city antiques dealers. Again it is the principle of moving things from one locality to another where they are more desirable. In this case from one area of appreciation to another.

All bedside tables and three-legged candlestands and tables are good, too, mainly because they will fit in the backseat of a car—which drop-leaf tables, for instance, won't do. And that makes them fast sellers for country antiques dealers catering to tourists. So all country dealers need them all the time. On the early ones—a little crudely made—don't touch that cracked and ratty-looking old finish. One such table, picked up for $300, was recently sold for $1,800 because it had a terribly deeply cracked original finish. But if the finish is just dull and dirty, it will pay simply to wash it off with denatured alcohol and some fine steel wool. And then give it a coat of lemon oil polish. That lemon oil smell is a great salesman. It makes people think of butlers and maids and rich little old ladies. Always use lemon oil to polish anything.

Game boards

As in going to the Ritz in Paris, France

Hot as a firecracker.

Oh, yes, there is money to be made in game boards, and this is because a lot of people haven't yet caught on to the fact that they are folk art, and we all know that folk art is worth whatever you have the nerve to ask for it. So you can still buy them for $45 to $65. And one famous price guide lists the very best of them for only around $350. Ha! Those really nicely

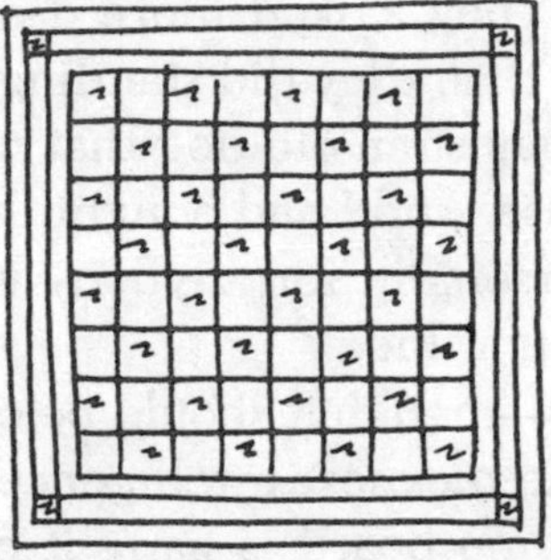

painted ones in bold colors are easily sold to rich stockbrokers who collect folk art for $750, and they will be worth twice that in three years the way the folk art market is moving these days.

What they are—most of them—are old breadboards that were discarded because they had gotten too dirty or smelly or whatever. So the farmhouse lady gave it to any old man who was hanging around to make a game board out of it. That's why most of them have the narrow brace strips on the end-grain edges to keep them from warping. Or trying to. It is the same thing that was done to the tops of country-made tables, which are called, naturally enough, breadboard-top tables.

I bought three of these once from a dealer at a large antiques flea market. He had them priced right at around $40 to $60 each. But while I was carrying them around under one arm, people started asking me if I wanted to sell them. So I just tacked $10 on to the price I had paid for each of them, and I made $30 and had my capital back in a half an hour.

Of course, there is a certain sales psychology involved there. They looked more desirable with me hugging them than they did standing on the ground propped up against an old dog that wasn't any good for anything else. And I had bought them, which was a sort of endorsement for anybody who was uncertain about their value.

Incidentally—though it should be obvious to those of you with the meanest intelligence—what you do with an old game board is hang it on your wall to show that you are a cultured person who knows enough to care about folk art. And often goes to New York City to study it at the Museum of American Folk Art on your way to the opera. I mean, folk art is ritzy. As in going to the Ritz—in Paris, France, that is.

Horses, horses, horses

All kinds of horses, and the effete rich people in Virginia

All horses sell. Some sell better than others, but they all sell. Wooden horses, stuffed horses, little horses on wheeled platforms, cast-iron horses and rocking horses. Sometimes rocking horses sell twice when some huckster splits one down the middle from nose to tail to make two separate wall hangings out of it. They do it with a tall band-saw or the kind you find at a shipyard or boat-building factory.

Other things being equal, you just can't lose buying a horse. Mark it up 15 to 25 percent and sell it

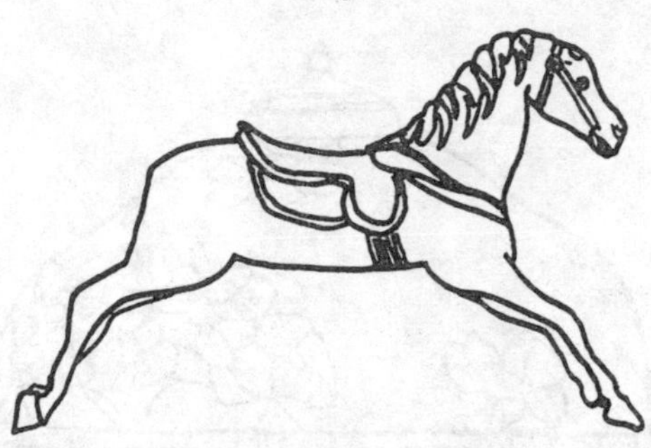

fast. But don't look in its mouth. You should never look in a horse's mouth. It's in bad taste.

Personally, I don't see why anyone would want a representation of a horse in his house. Horses are totally stupid and self-centered, and cowboys used to hate them. They are all strength and have almost no brains at all. They kick little children and bite romantic teenage girls not because they are cruel—but just because they are stupid. And people who get all excited about the totally unimportant fact that one can run faster than another around an oval track should have their heads examined. Boring. Boring. Boring.

Leaded glass

This comes in two shapes: in panels and in lamp shades.

The panels on the market today were originally windows in old churches of the early 1900s. Others come from libraries and big Victorian houses where they were used inside as dividers or were lit up from behind for gentle illumination.

These sell mostly to people who are starting restaurants or redecorating them. But lots of builders like to put them in new houses. So the people you should contact when you've located one are architects—who are listed in the Yellow Pages. So you call the whole list of them up on the telephone and tell them what you have. They will either need some at the time or not, and you can also ask them what other old house treasures they may need from time to time.

The money-making aspect of this is that architects are all big spenders, because the more a house costs, the more they make. So they won't flinch at paying twice what the windows cost you at some flea market. Maybe more.

The hanging lampshades made of leaded glass are an entirely different matter. In the Victorian era anyone who could afford to have a dining room table had one of these hanging over it. And today the simplest of the genuine ones is in the $1,500 and up class. A large one with many small pieces of glass could run you $65,000. If a product of the Tiffany Studios, $165,000.

But what you will see at the antiques flea markets (as opposed to the "old-toaster" flea markets) is a plethora of reproductions that are being handmade one at a time and mostly run from $350 for a small one to $650 to $800. So this is too much money to be investing unless you have already talked to a dealer who wants you to pick one up for him or her. In which case you have to arrive at a firm agreement about the exact size, design and colors that the dealer wants and that you get a 20 percent markup on a given price for finding and delivering the object. So in one week you can make $120 on a $600 investment. Which ain't hay. So maybe you will settle for making only $60.

Mission furniture

Where the big bucks are if you can buy it from your dentist

I realize that Mission furniture pieces are far too heavy for you to be hauling from auction house to dealer for your usual 20 or 25 percent markup. But if you can buy a piece from out of a dentist's office or from a Salvation Army store, how does a 1,000 percent markup sound to you? And this can happen because very few people in the general populace have heard about what has happened with Mission furniture in the last ten years.

Mission, of course, is that heavy oak-plank furniture of the early 1900s that is squared up and as ugly

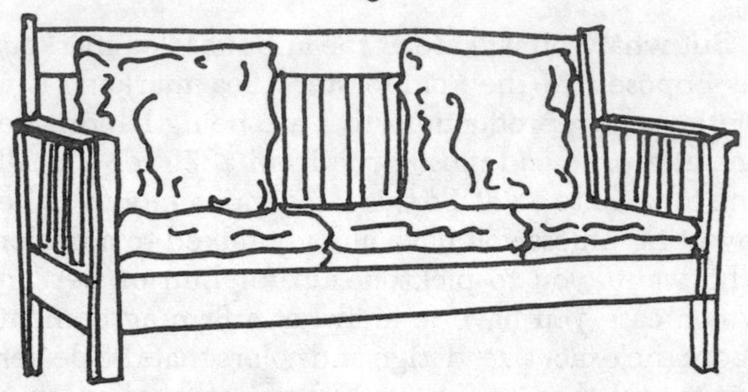

as a packing case for a locomotive. Though it usually has extra strong leather seats, which is more than you can say for most packing cases.

And while there was no call for it at all ten years ago, some Mission pieces are now bringing as much as $3,500 at auctions.

So the profit lies in buying pieces of Mission from people who don't know that Mission has been "discovered" by the effete intellectual rich who buy their furniture at Sotheby Park Bernet, the big New York City auction house. Or if they have heard about it think that is why you are giving them an amazing $600 for a piece of the old junk. Which happens to be worth a fast $1,500 to you. Even more if there is still a manufacturer's label on it showing that it was made by the factory of Gustave Stikly in upper New York state.

Oil paintings

Primitive, itinerant, ancestor, folk, and how to tell a good one

Now don't tell me you don't know anything about art. Because that is not what we are talking about. We

are talking about which paintings you should buy at auctions and flea markets that you can sell fast at a reasonable profit. And there is a way to decide that is so obvious that I am ashamed of you for not having thought of it yourself.

It is based on that old cliché, "I don't know anything about art, but I know what I like." Because it isn't art that makes a fast seller, but what people like. So all you have to do is look at a picture and decide, if someone gave it to you, would you have it in your house? Or would your mother or father like it? Or your Uncle John the fisherman, or Aunt Mary the baseball player? Or Tom your bartender? Would someone like it if you gave it to them as a present? So given that criterion you are not going to run across many paintings worth buying. There are a couple of million ancestor portraits out there, for instance, that are a drag on the market. Also the classical landscapes with a cow resting under a tree. So what you are looking for are pictures with an innocent or even ingenuous look of having been done by an amateur. As in primitive paintings, which were done by amateurs in the olden times when the rolling hills of our republic were still filled with cows and barns and farmhouses and dogs and cats. Homey. Grandma Moses.

In fact, amateur paintings from any time—such as the 1920s and 1930s—have a big appeal today. And the thing about amateur paintings is that they are not classified as to price the way paintings by any painter who has made a name for himself are. So you have those wonderful situations where somebody showing at a flea market thinks a painting he has for sale is worth $30 and you think it is worth $300, and with a difference of opinion that big, how can you go wrong? One thing to watch out for in these amateur/primitives is that, of course, it may go the other way around—with you thinking the painting is worth $30 and the owner thinking it is worth $300. So offer him $30, and see what he says. He may have just been looking for a sucker.

Another thing to watch out for in amateur/primitive paintings is that many aren't as great as they appear to be because they weren't done from nature or "real life" but were copied from steel-engraving black-and-white prints that somebody thought would look better in color. And this was a very popular practice with amateur artists and in young ladies' art schools.

There are also a lot of copies—very fine ones—of Italian Renaissance paintings around that were done by students in the Victorian era, which you should bring around to your interior decorator friends as they are considered great "camp" by a certain segment of our multifaceted populations.

Still another thing you have to watch out for are what seem to be wonderfully colorful paintings of flowers, fruits and rural scenes that look too good to be true. And they are. These are an early Victorian phenomenon and were widely distributed as advertising premiums. But on *very* close inspection you will see that they are very thin color-printed sheets of paper glued to and pressed into a cheap canvas so that the weave embosses the canvas. And it takes close inspection to perceive the hoax. These color prints were produced in Germany, which did the color printing for the world in the Victorian era. Postcards, too. And even the lithographed tin toys; thin sheets of tin were lithographed (printed) first, then pressed and cut into shape.

And finally, you can often make a real killing by buying and cleaning a dirty old painting that has so much smoke and soot on it that you can hardly see it because it hung in back of a kitchen wood stove for fifty years. And don't scream that you're not "handy," because it is the simplest and easiest thing to do in the world and I'm going to tell you how right now!

But before you will be able to believe me you will have to understand why it is so easy. And that is because the surface of virtually all oil paintings that you will ever find is covered with a coating of pure shellac. This was done by the original artist after the oils had dried for a few weeks to restore the wetness or luster to the colors that were lost as they dried out.

Denatured alcohol (which used to be called "wood alcohol") will quickly dissolve the shellac without disturbing the oil paint beneath it at all. Which is marvelous to watch happen because all the smoke, soot, grime and dirt is in the shellac coating.

The way you do this is by laying the painting face up on a work table and flooding the surface with a cup or more of the denatured alcohol, which you have bought at your paint and hardware store. Then you let this soak in until the shellac is completely dissolved—in about five minutes—which you determine by touching the surface with your fingertip. (And, of course, you have kept the surface flooded during the five minutes by adding liberal amounts of denatured alcohol.)

Finally, you stand the painting on edge and brush all the dirty shellac down onto the table—which I hope you had the sense to cover with ten layers of newspaper before you began. And you will be amazed at what has happened. You will feel like God must have right after He created the world. (No disrespect. God and I have been good friends since I was six.)

ONE MORE THING: You must do this in a well-ventilated room with two windows open and a fan going—or even better, outdoors in the summer on a picnic table—as the fumes from alcohol will give you a terrible headache and make you start to pass out. That is why they put the smell in denatured alcohol —so you will notice what is going on.

After the painting has thoroughly dried, you can put a fresh coat of shellac on it to help out the next fellow who has to clean it a hundred years from now. That is, if you are a nice person.

Photographs

The biggest sleeper out there in the marketplace

Here's another lesson in the psychology of selling.

The reason you can make good money in old photographs has very little to do with their inherent value based on their charm, beauty, historic significance or rarity. It is because of the way they are offered for sale at auctions and flea markets in big boxes full of them, which diminish by sheer quantity the value of them individually.

So if you are at a flea market and find a box full of photos being offered individually, what you do is pick out the five to ten most interesting of them and buy them. Then when you go to your dealer customers you only offer one of them. Even offering them in a group of four or five diminishes the value of all of them. The perceived value, that is.

If you have to buy a whole box at an auction, that's okay, too. You pick out the best for your stock and get rid of the rest of them by offering them to some flea market dealer for a price he can't refuse. And again, you offer the ones you have chosen only one at a time.

That's the sales technique. As to the value of each photograph, that has to be determined on two different levels. The first level concerns how you yourself react to the content of the photograph. If you find it interesting, someone else will, too. If you think it is valuable, someone else will, too. Especially if presented by you all by itself.

The other way of evaluating photographs is by the photographer who took it. Because this is the way collectors of old photographs evaluate them. So if the photograph is signed or the photographer is in some other way identified, you have found something that

may be of significant value—as in the hundreds of dollars, really rare ones in the low thousands.

If you are really interested in photographs, then you should make a specialty of them and learn something about the famous old photographers whose work is highly valued. And that's not hard either. The next time you see a dealer at an antique show that has a lot of photographs, just ask him for the names of the books he uses to evaluate his. Such a dealer will tell you because he has an interest in your becoming a source of supply for him. Dealers above all people understand that being secretive is for jerks, and making lots of contacts is the road to having more stuff to sell for more money. Ah, greed—the most powerful motivating force in the human psyche!

Also, photographs won't take up much space in your station wagon—or even the backseat. If you can just restrain yourself—showing only one at a time!

Picture books and blocks

Victorian children's books often had full-color pictures of ducks and other lovable farm animals on their covers. Similar color prints were also pasted on the outside of nesting blocks, often with panels as large as eighteen by eighteen inches.

Well, these are such a good thing and in such demand that you can easily mark them up 50 to 100 percent over what they go for at flea markets or went for at an auction. They are the kind of object whose

value lies in the eye of the beholder, and so you just have to offer them until you come to a beholder that really appreciates how decorative and historically artistic they are.

Portraits, country

Made in oils and watercolor by itinerant artists

During most of the 1800s portrait artists of widely varying talent roamed the countrysides of the whole East Coast in wagons full of cheap canvases, some of them with the backgrounds already painted in but blank spaces left for the head and top part of the body. That was something to do to keep busy in the winter months when it was too cold to travel around in the wagons.

Most of these artists made oil paintings whose charm is based on a certain innocence about the craft of drawing. And the value of any one of them is pretty much in the eye of the beholder. Which makes

them a good class of object to buy and sell at a profit if you have any pretensions to artistic taste. Which means only that you have definite ideas about what is good or bad, or even about what you like and don't like.

One tip I can give you about these—and all oil paintings—is that, generally speaking, they sell better without frames than with them. I think this is because without frames they look more like a discovery just found in some old lady's attic. But there is also the factor that the framed ones usually have terrible frames on them, frames whose color has no relationship to the colors used in the painting. Frames that were just put on because they fit and pictures are supposed to have frames on them.

The watercolor portraits made by itinerant artists offer a special opportunity for making money for all of the above reasons plus the fact that they look so faded, dusty and fragile that people in their right minds would never guess how much they are worth to collectors of this sort of thing. And we are talking about a price range of $1,000 to $2,500 for things that look just terrible.

Quilts

Where bold colors put you in the $1,000 to $2,000 range

Quilts have recently become a good item to trade in because they have been discovered by interior

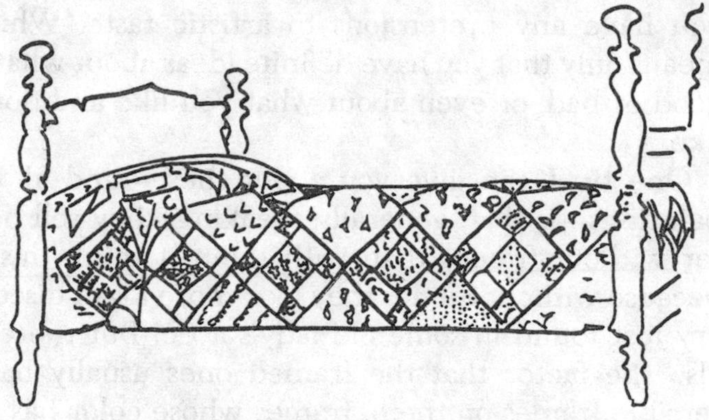

decorators, the less expensive being put on beds, the really colorful and valuable ones being stitched to heavy cloth and hung on walls. So you can sell them directly to the interior decorators instead of to antique dealers, keeping your share of the profits higher. Even the furniture departments of good department stores will be delighted to see what you have and take a steady stream of them off your hands.

The best ones, of course, are those with the

brightest and boldest colors. Which brings us to the Amish quilts, which are the cream of the crop, and you will need a book about quilts to get familiar with what is desirable. The full-color Knopf collectors' guide to quilts is the best I have ever seen.

Speaking of colorful, the quilts made by the Amish people in Pennsylvania are works of art, and many people collect them. But since the Amish are still turning them out at a good clip, this brings us to an interesting area where antiquity is combined with folk art. So that even the ones that are currently being made by the Amish for sale outside of their community cost almost as much as the older ones. And while you will need a price guide, we are talking in the $1,000 to $2,000 range.

Worth mentioning is that quilts don't take up any noticeable room in your station wagon, and in an emergency you can sleep under them to keep warm while you are waiting for some flea market to open.

Signs

From tavern boards to Burma Shave, you can't go wrong

Everybody loves signs. People even steal them all the time. Even brand new ones. Even directional signs and street signs that are supposed to help people get where they are going. I mean, what respectable game room doesn't boast at least one stolen sign presided over by the idiot who tells you where he

stole it? But, of course, that is the secret of why signs are so popular: they can be used as interior decoration by just hanging them on your wall. And objects that can be used in interior decorations have an edge on everything else. They are especially effective when a group of small antique ones are displayed on a wall. And not only in game rooms.

At the top of the line would be hand-painted swinging board Early American tavern signs, which belong in a museum and go for from $5,000 to $15,000. Which either of us should be lucky enough to find. But if you ever did find one, the best way to get your highest profit on it would be to take it to one of the top New England or New York City auctioneers, who get the highest prices for this sort of thing. These are the houses that advertise their auctions in the trade press, such as *The Maine Antique Digest.* Phillips, Sotheby, Doyle, Bourne, Julia, Withington, et cetera.

But the meat and potatoes of the old sign business are old store signs dating right up through the early 1900s. The value of these lies in the fact that they are hand-lettered, making each one unique and certainly a second cousin at least to folk art, which means that their value lies in the eye of the beholder. By which I especially mean that somebody named Horton is going to lust a lot harder for a sign that says HORTON BROS. DYE WORKS than anybody not named Horton. So use your telephone book to find somebody rich in your area named Horton and sell it to him for twice what an antique dealer would give you for it. Or twice what a dealer would ask for a similar sign.

The same principle operates with a sign that has a town name in it. Go sell it in that town. Or if you find a sign for the Howe Scale Co., and you find out that the Howe Scale Company has been in Rutland, Vermont, for the last hundred years and is still going—which is true—are you going to try to sell that to somebody named Grotz? Or are you going to take it to Rutland and sell it to one of the executives at the plant up there? Or even just send the president of the company a Polaroid of it. To buy with company money to hang in his office, and take home with him when he retires or whatever. In fact, he is probably still named Howe, or his wife's father was. Or somebody is.

And, as I said earlier, this thing of moving things to where people especially value them is one of the basic money-making principles of the whole business.

At the bottom of the line are the enamel advertising signs. But having been mass-produced, they are so plentiful that their value has been pretty firmly established with the result that there is little chance of your making any noticeable money on them.

But if you could find me a weathered wooden street sign reading MONTEGO ST., now that would be a find, wouldn't it. You could sell that to any rich writer in a flash. Maybe even to a literate Doubleday editor.

Ah, the joy of antiques is in old signs if it is anywhere! And *big* fast profits, too.

Statuettes, metal

The opportunity in buying and selling metal statuettes lies in the fact that the good brass and bronze ones don't look very different from the ones made of "white metal"—which is actually a lead alloy like

pewter. At least they don't look much different after bronze-colored finishes have been put on them by various means.

Of course, the difference can be clearly established by scratching the bottom of the object with a pointed knife. The "lead" shines brightly through like silver.

So the opportunity lies, of course, in your learning to tell the difference and finding a real brass one among the lead ones at some flea market.

Stoneware

The crocks and jugs that every dealer needs at least one of

The value of a stoneware crock is determined by how unusual the decoration on it is. Bob Bonner found one somewhere in upstate New York once that had an elephant on it. And since there is only one other known that has an elephant on it, he estimated it to be worth $3,500. And it was. And has since been sold for considerably more. But what the heck, you can't win them all.

And there are a lot of things made out of stoneware besides crocks. All kinds of jugs and jars. Which when they are red are called, of all things, redware. And yellow, yellowware, et cetera.

As to the problem of making money buying and selling these, they are a good standard item to deal in, and their price guide values are pretty well known. There are several price guides to them, and

they are well covered in the Knopf series of price guides to antiques that I keep suggesting you buy because they are a university education in the whole field of American antiques (you can order them through any intelligent bookstore even if they are not carried in stock).

So you don't buy crocks from flea market dealers that have a lot of them. They will know very well how much each of them is worth. But when you see a dealer with only one of them, offer him half of what he is asking for it. Best of all find one at a garage sale or one of those junky flea markets that specialize in old pots and pans and used toasters. Because the people who sell at such places rarely realize the value of ironstone or any other kind of pottery.

Only buy ironstone and similar items at an auction unless a lot of it is being offered—say, more than a dozen pieces. The first ones will go highest because all the dealers there will need a piece or two to round out their stock. And after they have gotten theirs, the going, going, gone price will go down far enough for

you to make a profit when taking what you have bought to dealers who weren't at the auction.

Store things

Oh, how those rich people love coffee mills and tin bins

All rich people have well-decorated kitchens; I mean people who live in those houses you see in *House & Garden.* And they all need one of those big coffee grinders that have big cast-iron wheels. They are all painted red as far as I know, with gold striping.

So you are pretty safe in buying these even at the relatively high price given in your favorite price guide, for resale to a big-city interior decorator.

You do this by looking up their names under "Interior Decorators & Designers" in the Yellow Pages of a

big-city telephone book. Then you call them on the telephone, which also gives you a chance to ask them about the kind of things they are looking for. Which you write down next to their names in the notebook you naturally have because you are an organized person.

Just tell them your price and stick to it—a good 30 percent over what you paid for it. When they try to get you to come down, tell them that you haven't called your whole list of prospects yet. In a few days they will start calling you back and asking you to bring it around so they can look at it. And then you've got them, because they asked to see it at your price.

So, of course, when you go, you bring any other goodies that you have at the time, and since you have come at their request, the pressure is on them to buy something else to encourage you to keep coming to them first with your merchandise. They know you came to them first because you tell them so. You tell them all so.

Other store things that rich people like for their kitchens are the big tin bins that coffee and sugar and

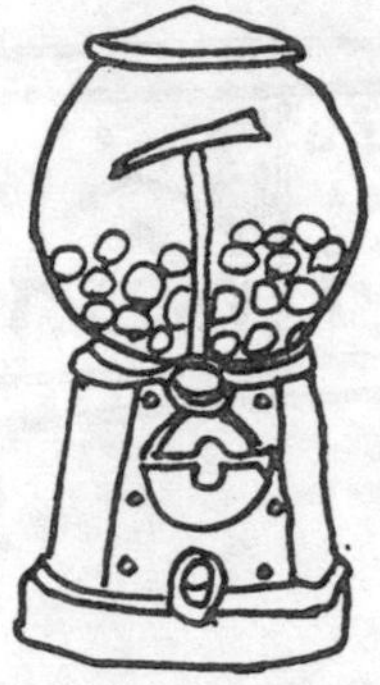

grains were kept in. They are usually painted black with nice little paintings of rural scenes on the front.

All of which illustrates two principles of successful dealing in the antiques business: Think interior decoration. Think rich people.

Stoves, small iron

The nice thing about little iron stoves is the way they just sit there. They're stable. They know who they are, and will accept no argument about it. They represent the days when Americans knew exactly who they were, and the little round stoves burned coal and the long ones were designed to take two-foot-long pieces of small trees, which obviously wouldn't fit into a small round one.

The important thing about the little round ones is that the grate isn't missing. The grate holds the coal up so that air can get under it.

The long wood-burning ones have no grate. But it

is good to put a couple of fire-bricks in them to make it easier to get the logs you are using burning. And if the bottom is beginning to rust out, have some pieces of sheet iron cut to fit in it. One piece is too big to get through the door.

At a country flea market or country auction these often go for $40 to $50. But once you have scrubbed some of the rust off with a wire brush from your friendly hardware store and spray-painted them dull black, you have an object that is worth $150 in an antique shop. About $50 of which should be your profit.

That's for the average small stove. But if you find one that is really low, long and narrow, it may be a very early one and therefore worth $600 or more to an old stove collector. The ordinary ones sell well to department stores and florists, who like to use them as display pieces.

Teddy bears

Would you believe that some of them have longer arms than others—and that that makes all the difference!

Teddy bears—named after Teddy Roosevelt, of course—have two things going for them. Not only does everybody like them, but there is also a growing group of people who collect them. People who aren't satisfied with just one teddy bear, but want to own twenty or thirty of them—which is driving their price up as these collectors fight over them.

But there is also something else you should know about teddy bears. And that is while your average old-looking teddy bear is worth $40 to $50 to a lot of people, there is also a special group of teddy bears that are worth a lot more—in the low hundreds. And these are the teddy bears that have long arms. True. I jest you not. The reason for this is that these are the oldest ones, which first came out right after Teddy Roosevelt shot his big grizzly bear that he had stuffed and is still around in some museum. Probably the

Smithsonian. It was an enormous bear, and after he had it stuffed, old T.R. used to like to go in a room with it all alone—just him and his bear—and meditate with it about life and death and all that. T.R. did most of the meditating, of course. The bear already knew all about it.

Tin toys

The early ones that were lithographed in Germany drive collectors crazy

Personally, little tin windup toys fascinate me. Which only goes to show my good taste, because they are the aristocracy of the antique toy business.

They were made by lithographing tin sheets that were then die-cut and embossed into shape before being assembled by hand by means of the little bendable tabs. This was all done in Germany—like the postcards of the era—from around 1905 right

through the 1940s. In the 1930s the Japanese got into the act, and with a temporary suspension of activity during the 1940s are still at it.

Now, I know that the value of all of these is firmly established by auctions held frequently by two big auction houses that specialize in them. So they are not the kind of object where the value is so uncertain that we are always looking for it. But the kind of flea market exhibitors who usually deal in old toasters and waffle irons are amazingly ignorant of the fact that many of these are worth in the hundreds of dollars. All of them pre-1940, rare early ones in the thousands.

I don't know if there is a price guide especially for these, but any of the general price guides to antiques will list a good many of these tin toys to give you a pretty good idea of what is what.

U.S. stamps

Revealing the big secret about them that even antique dealers don't know (worth the price of this book again!)

Never tear or soak a stamp off an old envelope.

Never tear or soak an old stamp from its envelope.

Never, never, never, never.

By doing so you will decrease the value of the stamp by an average of 66 2/3 percent. Stamp collectors are not ninnies, and have all kinds of appreciation of the aesthetics and history which are involved in the envelope the stamp was on.

The same thing goes for stamp albums. You don't take the good stamps out of it and throw the ratty old album away. Stamp collectors like old albums with their stamps in them, too.

Now as to the reason why old envelopes with stamps and old stamp albums are good things to buy and sell at a profit to stamp dealers. And the answer is that to all but one antique dealer in two hundred they are a mystery that they think is an impenetrable one, and so they just don't bid on them. I know this because at auction after auction when I have bid on an old album or bunch of old letters, never more than one person in the audience has bid against me. And we all had the opportunity to look at the stamps at the preview of the auction.

But you can become a comparative expert in stamps in only a couple of hours spent in your library checking out the bible of old stamps, *The Scott Catalogue of U.S. Stamps,* which contains pictures of all of them. And the unknown reason that this is possible is that there are only about a hundred different designs on them that are worth over $10. (Each design comes in different colors and denominations, which make for relatively small variations in value.) And there are only fifty designs that are worth over $50. And you can easily become familiar with these in a couple of hours.

Amazing, but true. However, I have to point out to you also that the prices given in the *Scott Catalogue* are double the actual value of the stamps. This is apparent if you look at the weekly newspaper of the stamp trade called *Linn's Stamp Review*, which your stamp dealer will let you look at if you are interested.

Obviously, mistakes in the printing process make such stamps exceptionally valuable. For instance, about $150,000 if you find a nice twenty-four-cent airmail stamp with the black biplane upside down inside the red frame.

Wagons and sleighs

As window decorations

Did you know that there really was an old wooden-runner sleigh with the trademark *Rosebud* on it?

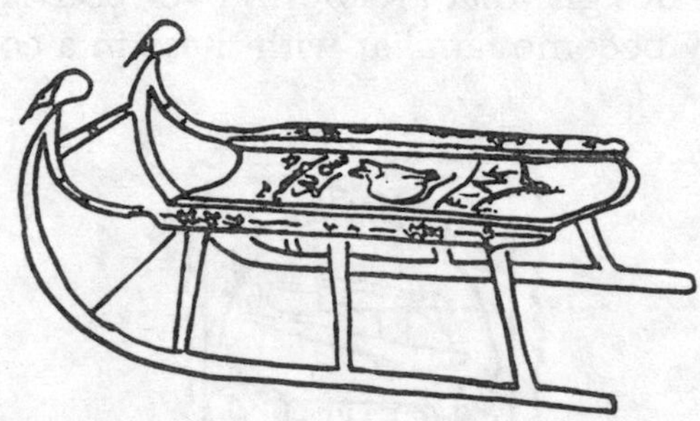

And because they burned one in the movie *Citizen Kane,* if you find one it is worth lots of thousands of dollars. Which means that the right place to sell it is through one of the big New York City auction houses. Which will sell it to some Hollywood mogul or other rich person. (I wonder if these are being faked yet? Or at least being honestly reproduced?)

But ordinary wooden sleighs and wagons of about that size can also be profitable. This is because there is a special demand for them outside the general marketplace for antiques. And this is for use as props in the window displays of "high"-class specialty shops and department stores. Not that the managers of these stores are going to go crazy about them, but they will pay good prices.

Weathervanes

The big thing that you have to understand—and ethically accept if you are going to make any money in the antiques business—is that the reality you per-

ceive is the reality you have got. Meaning, of course, that most antique copper weathervanes you will ever see are fakes, but if everybody out there is selling them to each other as authentic old ones, that's the only game in town and who are we to not play ball with the rest of the fellows.

The reason for this lies in the way these hollow sheet copper figures of horses and cows and roosters were made in the first place. And is still so easy to do now in the second place.

They are made by pounding sheets of copper into a pair of hollow molds with a leather mallet and other smaller instruments. The matching sides are then trimmed with metal-cutting shears and are soldered together. The molds used to be hand-carved blocks of hard wood. Today the molds are made of fiberglass and resin of the kind sold for waterproofing the bottoms of old boats. It is a tricky, sticky process of wrapping the resin-soaked fiberglass around an authentic, well-greased old weathervane. And when removed, the pair of impressions are then backed up by pressing them into wet concrete.

This is being done so widely now that some makers are selling their weathervanes while the copper is still bright and the soldered edges still shiny. There is not a lot of profit to be made on these because the prices are standard. Unless, of course, you have previously spoken to one of the dealers you are buying for and you have previously agreed with him on how much he will give you for finding it and bringing it to him. Say a 15 percent markup over what you have to pay. And maybe buy a couple more on speculation to try to peddle to any antique shops you may pass on your way home. And if you have to sell them for what you paid to get your capital back in operation. And you will at least have talked to a few more dealers to find out what they are looking for to buy from you the next time you are in the neighborhood.

The faking part comes when these fresh reproductions are dipped in some acid to create a surface patina that looks a hundred years old. And then you shoot a couple of .22 bullets through them from an angle to simulate their having been shot at from the ground while they were still on some old barn.

The prices for these are given in some detail in lots of price guides, but you are dealing in the $1,500 to $15,000 price range so there are certainly good amounts of money to be made. By this I mean that if you only get a 15 percent markup when selling it to a dealer, that's $225, and any good dealer is anxious to get one because they move like hotcakes.

As far as my telling you the name of the acid you

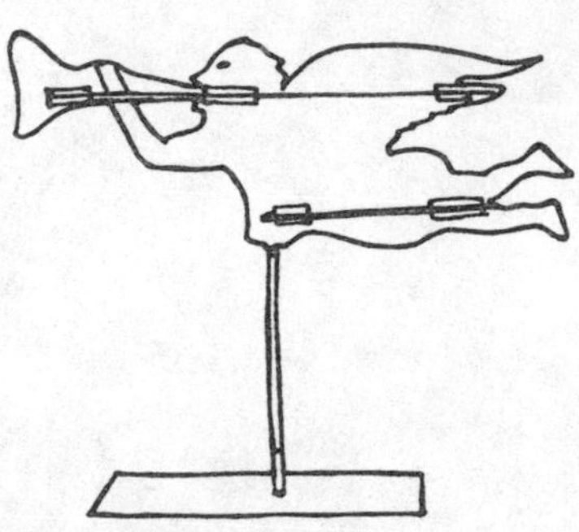

dip the brand-new-looking reproductions in goes, my lawyer tells me that my doing so would make me equally guilty with you if somebody ever sued you for selling a fake. But it is a pretty commonly sold acid and you can find out easily enough if you really want to. And even a crook like you can protect himself by keeping a good, clear carbon of the receipt you give your customer that says on it, "Appears to be circa 1890 [or 1910, or whatever] but authenticity not guaranteed by seller." Oh, how the law does favor the criminal class!

Part III

24 THINGS NOT TO BUY

24 Things Not to Buy

They may look interesting to you, maybe to everybody, but they just don't sell

I knew a dealer back in Connecticut who was a wonderful man. He was a retired foreign correspondent who used to know Erich Remarque—who wrote *All Quiet on the Western Front.* You meet all kinds of fascinating people in the antiques business. It's a fringe benefit.

GRAVESTONES

Anyway, some picker had brought him one of the best hand-carved gravestones you ever saw. A true work of art, with some funny verse, which I forget. But he had had it in his shop for years, and by the time I saw it, the price was down to 15 cents. He told me, "Everybody admires it, but nobody wants death in their house."

HEARSES

Which is why beautiful, shiny old hearses are also a drug on the market. And early photographs of babies in their little coffins—spare me!

STAINED GLASS

Religious things don't move well either. Stained glass from old churches will sell if you already know somebody that is calling for it. But if there is a picture of a saint or Mary or Jesus in it, it won't sell at all, because people are afraid of appearing sacrilegious.

POTTY CHAIRS

A third area of things that have undesirable connotations is represented by potty chairs. These are straight chairs in the Boston Rocker style and at one point every bedroom had one. They have a hole in the seat and a box under it to hold the "thunder mug." Even with a pillow on the seat, you can still see the box, and nobody wants one in their living room. And even if you have a cabinetmaker take the box out, nobody wants to pay you enough for your time spent fooling around with the poor thing. Obviously, you can also forget the "thunder mugs" that went in them. And anything else related to this undignified aspect of our lives.

CHILDREN'S CHAIRS

Children's antique chairs—people want clean new ones for their children, and grown-ups can't use them.

HANGING LAMPS

Victorian hanging-from-the-ceiling oil lamps. No call for them except in the Midwest, and not very strong there either.

EMPIRE FURNITURE

Band-saw Empire. Chunky pine in simple curves covered with mahogany veneer. The only place people want it is in the South, especially Georgia, because it is the style Southerners furnished their new houses with after Sherman proved that war is Hell. And it is too much trouble for you to soak it in a lake to get the veneer off, reglue the parts, cut off some curves, refinish it and sell it for "country pine"—though this was a widespread practice some years ago.

FIDDLES

Every few years some musician who knows his fiddles will buy one—but they won't move for you so don't tie even $5 of your capital in one.

CHIPPED CHINA

Any China or glass that is chipped—won't sell for pennies. No dealer wants it. Of course, you could take it home to use yourself.

GLASS DOMES

Straw flowers under glass domes. Even just the glass domes. Takes too long to find someone who wants one.

BIRDS

Mounted dead birds—no call. But a stuffed chicken in a basket—for some reason, these are a hot item—will sell in a shop for as high as $50 to $60.

FISH

Mounted dead fish. Blah.

RELIGIOUS THINGS

Bibles and other religious things such as altar cloths and incense burners are also guaranteed non-sellers. They may be of value to somebody someplace, but not in antique shops. The dealers have a nice term for such things; they call them shelf sitters.

PATTERN GLASS, ETC.

Other shelf sitters are pattern glass, cut glass, old tools, old kitchenware and flatware.

ENCYCLOPEDIAS

You can also forget old encyclopedias. Though the 1911 Eleventh Edition of the Britannica is still worth around $40 in the fine print edition and $100 in the Jumbo edition at retail. But that is the only one that is worth anything.

FANCY BRASS

Scientific instruments and brass telescopes are nice-looking, but the trouble is that there isn't any market for them. Just try to think of the last time you saw one in an antique shop. There may be a market for them somewhere, but it is too narrow a corner for you to waste time trying to find it.

SCRIMSHAW

Carved whales' teeth and other scrimshaw. Same as above—too narrow a market, as narrow as New Bedford. And your chance of getting stuck with a fake is very large. Probably 80 percent of all you will ever see are fakes. Even if everybody makes believe they are real just to keep the ball rolling.

SAMPLERS

Stitched samplers in frames. Dark, dirty and depressing. Even if you could resell them, you wouldn't want to talk to the kind of people who buy them.

SPITTOONS

Spittoons. Ladies have no sense of humor when it comes to interior decorating their nests. None.

TOOLS

Dark, dirty, rusty tools and kitchen utensils. There is a weird part of our population that thinks these are great. So let them be happy with each other.

COLLECTOR PLATES

Recently manufactured "collector's" plates of supposedly limited editions that are supposed to rapidly climb in value are just a bad joke. The whiskey bottles, too.

SILVER BOWLS

Silver bowls are always good shelf sitters. I guess everybody already has a silver bowl that they got for a wedding present.

CLOCKS

Shelf and mantelpiece clocks naturally have value, but only to a narrow segment of our population, and every antique shop already has some—that they like to sell to *you*.

VICTROLAS

Phonographs and Victrolas are too heavy and always overvalued by the people who are trying to sell them.

THE END. Now go out there and buy "the right stuff."

And so it goes, as Kurt Vonnegut always says.

This only touches the surface of what you shouldn't buy. The principle is that being interesting doesn't mean that an object will resell. It should also be decorative and the kind of thing people will want to decorate with. Because that is what fast-moving antiques are all about. Not dark things, or tiny things or just old or just dead things, but antiques you can decorate with, as I always say.

APPENDIX

References

Price Guides

There are over a hundred of these to every kind of antique and collectible that you can imagine. And they are useful to specialists. But you will quickly find out about them when you get interested in some specialty. The only one you really need for general dealing is "Warman's," as it is popularly known:

Antiques and Their Prices, by E. G. Warman, which is available in almost all bookstores.

But if you really want to know something about antiques in depth, you should look into the Knopf series of price guides, which are fully illustrated in gorgeous color and give lots of information about each object that very much relates to their market value.

Available through any good bookstore, these come in separate volumes: *Furniture, Glass, Dolls, Folk Art, Silver, Toys, Pottery* and *Quilts.* This series is as close as you will ever get to a university education in antiques. It is available by mail order from *The Antiques and Arts Weekly* (see listing below) and if you write to them, they will send you the pertinent information. Write to the editor, genial R. Scudder Smith.

Trade Papers

These are tabloid-sized newspapers in which people in the trade advertise to each other. They also have photo stories on lots of auctions and report the prices things went for and sometimes why. *The Maine Antique Digest* basically serves the Northeast; *The Antiques and Arts Weekly* basically serves the market within a 150-mile radius of New York City, as well as the international market in New York City; and *The Antiques Trader Weekly* serves the Midwest. They will all send you a sample copy for $1.

The Maine Antique Digest. Sally Pennington, Box 358, Waldoboro, Maine 04572. This is the indispensable one for anybody who wants to make money in antiques. It is jammed full of ads and editorial stuff about the kinds of things I have talked about in this book.

The Antiques and Arts Weekly. R. Scudder Smith, Editor, Bee Publishing Company, Newtown, Connecticut 06470. Covers the greatest marketplace for antiques and old art in the world. The best stuff, the expensive stuff, but also all the antique shows and auctions in the area.

The Antiques Trader Weekly. Box 1050, Dubuque, Iowa 52001. Covers the Midwest like a blanket the same way *The Maine Antique Digest* covers the Northeast. And just as indispensable if you live in the Midwest.

Books

There are thousands of books about antiques, but when it comes to books about the antiques business, there is only one worth your time or money. It is *How to Be Successful in the Antiques Business* by Ron S. Barlow. And if you are serious about making money in antiques, it is worth ten times the $12.95 plus $1 for postage and handling that it will cost you. Send your check or money order to Windmill Publishing Co., 2147 Windmill View Road, El Cajon, California 92020. The book is a veritable encyclopedia of specific information on all aspects of the business and totally oriented to making money in it. It was a best-seller in the business a few years ago, but if you hurry, there may be a copy left for you.